Center Time

A Complete Guide to Learning Centers

by Dana McMillan

illustrated by Kathryn Marlin and Janet Armbrust

Teaching & Learning Company

1204 Buchanan St., P.O. Box 10
Carthage, IL 62321

This book belongs to

Tina M. Simoneau

Cover by Kathryn Marlin

Copyright © 1994, Teaching &
Learning Company

ISBN No. 1-57310-007-2

Printing No. 9876

Teaching & Learning Company
1204 Buchanan St., P.O. Box 10
Carthage, IL 62321

Table of Contents

Table of Contents

Why Use Learning Centers?

Designing an early childhood classroom that incorporates learning centers provides a learning experience that is developmentally appropriate for the following reasons:

Young children learn best in an environment that allows them to interact with other children. In learning centers children work in small groups with materials that are interesting to them and in an environment which promotes communication about learning.

Young children gain very little from a lecture format where an adult talks at them. They learn from direct experiences where they can demonstrate as they work with interesting materials. Well-designed learning centers provide a rich variety of materials for children to manipulate.

Young children need time to work on problems they find interesting. They do not need to hurry through one paper and pencil task that only leads to another. When learning centers are the structure for the classroom, and ample time is provided for work in centers, children can become deeply involved in a process that they find challenging and interesting.

Young children find it challenging and rewarding to make choices about their work for the day. Even if they work for long periods of time, children are more attentive and tend to have fewer traditional problems with staying on task and working productively when they feel they have some control over their learning and actions.

In a learning center structure, young children look forward to their time in school, make plans about their own learning for the next school day and are very confident about telling others what they learned.

Many schools are engaged in serious discussions about outcomes for students. The outcomes described above are often on the list of ones we want for all students. This book will help you design a program that begins this process in the early years. Research tells us the benefits will last a lifetime.

Developmentally Appropriate Progam and Learning Centers

The following concepts are taken from the widely acclaimed position statement from the **National Association for the Education of Young Children (NAEYC)**, 1986 and how they apply to learning centers:

Developmentally Appropriate Programs

- *Understand that children develop best through activities that capture their interest.* Learning centers should be designed with materials that are interesting to young children. Blocks, painting, books, dress-up clothes, and science materials found in nature are enticing to young children and provide a focus for their learning.

- *Understand that the most important role of the early childhood educator is to create an environment in which children can make discoveries, solve problems and think independently.* Learning centers provide a structure for children to develop these critical skills. When children decide which center to work in, or what to do when an area is full, they are learning to solve the types of problems they will face for the rest of their lives.

- *Provide a well-designed learning environment, filled with a rich variety of materials for children to manipulate.* Carefully chosen materials, labeled in a way that makes sense to young children, and facilitation of a teacher who knows how to encourage children's discoveries, make this concept closely related to learning centers.

- *Accept that children progress through the same stages of development but at their own individual pace.* Well-designed learning centers allow children at a variety of stages of development to use the same materials in ways that are meaningful and appropriate for them.

- *Recognize the most effective way to evaluate a child's progress is through ongoing observation and informal assessment.* In a learning center classroom, teachers have time to work with small groups of children in the centers and make very important observations about their development.

Chapter 1
Developmentally Appropriate Program

Books About Cats

Books About Flowers

Books About Clowns

The Three- to Seven-Year-Old Child

Known as the pre-operational child, this is an interesting and unusual thinking child. Understanding how this child thinks is critical to structuring a learning center classroom that is appropriate.

For the pre-operational child, language is the dramatic attainment. Between the ages of three and seven the child develops a significant amount of vocabulary. Communication of thoughts and ideas is developing and needs to be stimulated and encouraged. Placing labels and developing categories are major processes during this age.

The social aspect of the child from three to seven is still primarily egocentric, but it is becoming more and more interactive during this stage. Children begin to work out their own problems, when given opportunities to do so. This social knowledge is developed when children interact with adults and other children. For this reason, social development is closely linked to the development of language.

Another major development of the pre-operational child is the ability to represent what has been learned or discovered. This new thinking is a result of the development of logic. Children have figured out that objects stay the same. In addition, they have learned that something other than the object can be used to represent the object. This allows the child to play in a symbolic manner–draw, paint, use objects to represent something else.

Learning Centers
and the Three- to Seven-Year-Old Child

In creating a learning center classroom, the most helpful information we can draw on is the information about the pre-operational child. For this reason, the classroom for this age child will look and operate in some ways that are different from classrooms for older children.

Language Development

The opportunity for language development in learning centers is endless. Besides being the obvious place for books, a Language Center (and other areas) offers experiences in the printed word, conversations, documenting work in print and seeing print in the environment. A well-designed center should include many opportunities for reading, writing and spoken language.

Social Development

Young children develop social skills in every center where interaction and problem solving is allowed. The Dramatic Play Center is just one place where this type of development is available for children. Social skills are obtained in block play, discussing art ideas, arguing over a puzzle piece, sharing a snack, singing a song, reading a story and many other group activities.

Representation

When young children work in centers like the Block, Art or Manipulative Center, they are often showing or representing what they know. Their block buildings demonstrate what they have learned about the school, their house or an airport. Their craft projects can show their understanding of form and structure, their manipulative work often allows a play representation of real world situations.

Play: The Learning Experience

One of the most misunderstood aspects of the activity created in a learning center classroom is that the children look as if they are playing. When we say that play is a child's work, what we may really mean is that play is an opportunity for learning. The issue then is to explain, to anyone who may not understand, how a child learns through play.

Begin with a definition of *play* . . .

Play is intrinsically motivated.

Play is relatively free of external rules.

Play is enacted as if the activity were real.

Play is focused on the process.

Play is dominated by the players.

Play requires that all of the players are actively involved.

If the activity is somewhat noisy, requires children to move around freely and does not produce a product suitable for framing on the refrigerator, chances are parents will need an explanation about what their child has gained that they cannot have on a Saturday at the park.

Stages of Play

Play develops in six increasingly complex stages. These stages will often be apparent as you observe children in learning centers.

1. **Unoccupied:** Children watch others at play but do not enter the play. Unoccupied children may just stand around or move about the learning centers.

2. **Onlooker:** Children watch others play, may talk to them or ask questions, and move closer to the group.

3. **Solitary:** The child plays alone with the materials even if others are sharing the same area. He doesn't change his play or interact with the others.

4. **Parallel:** A child uses the materials like those nearby. The child does not try to influence the other children's activities. She plays beside rather than with the other children.

5. **Associative:** Common activities occur between children. They may exchange materials. Everyone in the group does similar things, but there are no specific roles or shared goals.

6. **Cooperative:** Children cooperate with others in the group to construct or produce something. The group is often defined by one or two leaders who see that the project is completed.

Adapted from *Play in the Lives of Children*, Rogers and Sawyers, AEYC.

Learning Center Vocabulary

The vocabulary that will be used in this book is described below.

Learning Center: The physical space in the room that is set aside for children to interact with other children and manipulate materials in small, informal settings.

Task or Materials: Materials added to learning centers that promote open-ended, interactive types of exploration by children.

Class Meeting: A group meeting held before the work time when children discuss the plans they have for their work at learning centers.

Work Time: The time when children and teachers are working in the learning centers. May also be called center time.

Review Time: The time immediately after work time when the children discuss the work time activity, discussing what they accomplished and what they plan to follow up with at the next session.

Management Plan: A plan developed by the teachers that includes decisions about how children will use learning centers, report their work and move between centers.

DAP 7

Chapter 2
Management Issues

What Is the Management Plan?

The management plan tells each person who is involved with your classroom how the children use the classroom learning centers. It is designed by the teacher with consideration to the developmental ages and stages of the children who live and learn in the environment. It should be a well-designed plan that makes sense to the teacher, children and parents.

Imagine running an office without a plan for who sits where, lunch schedules, hours for work and job responsibilities.

Translate that same concept to the classroom and think about a plan to organize your classroom for using learning centers. A management plan should answer the following questions for the children:

- What does the teacher expect from me during the time I am working in the centers?

- What are my options for work to be done?

- Who will be working with me?

- How long may I stay at each area?

- How will I know when the time is over?

- What are my responsibilities when we finish with our center work?

Management Plan Evaluation Form

Use this form to evaluate your needs for a management plan.

I am interested in having learning centers in my classroom because _____

_____

_____

_____

I want children in my classroom to be able to _____ as a result
of their experience with learning centers.

It is important that my room be_____

_____

It is important that my room not be _____

_____

My role in the classroom during center time will be to _____

_____

_____

_____

(Put a star by the ones that may be difficult for you to do.)

To make learning centers work in our school, I will need to consult the following people:

_____

Child Choice vs. Teacher Control

Children need to feel as if they have some opportunities in their *daily* routine where they are allowed to make decisions. Learning centers are a method for allowing children to have choices, if your management plan provides for choice.

All of us have a need to have control over some portion of our lives.

Consider:

- You attend an educational conference where every minute of the day is scheduled for you with just enough time between sessions.

- On your vacation the tour bus makes frequent stops that are carefully planned for you, even down to the decision about where and what you will have for lunch.

  At the end of the day how do you feel?

Vs.

- A day where you have a number of errands to run and things to accomplish, but it's up to you to decide how and in what order you will get them all done.

  At the end of the day how do you feel?

Children feel the same way about the need for some control of their own schedule.

Planning for Learning Centers

One of the most effective methods for allowing children to have meaningful choices is to let them make plans for their work during a learning center time.

Your management plan can allow children to feel as if they have some control if you allow them to make some of the following decisions:

- Choose the learning center where they will work first.

- Describe a specific activity or project to be completed.

- Invite another child or small group of children to work together.

- Decide when they are ready to move to another area in the room.

- Take materials designed for one use and create another way to use them.

- Choose to stay with one activity for the entire learning center period.

Examples of Times When Children Make Real Choices	Examples of Times When Teachers Make Real Choices
Children decide what to play outside during a recess period.	The teacher picks the captains and allows the children to choose the teams for a game at recess.
Children choose books to check out of the library.	The teacher chooses the book to read for story time.
Children pick a puzzle from a selection stored on a shelf at the Manipulative Center.	The teacher puts one puzzle at each table for each small group of children to work together.
A child decides on an art project, chooses materials at the Art Center and completes it.	The children make an art project by following a model and step-by-step directions so that each finished product looks the same.
Each child follows an individual recipe to make a snack as an optional center during work time.	Snack time is a scheduled period where children sit together and are served their portions of the food.
Gym class is organized with stations where children may choose an area to work for the period.	Gym class is a series of teacher-directed games and activities.

Schedule Formula

How much of your day should you allow for children to have some choices in their schedule, activities and with whom they will work?

The formula on the next page will help you make this decision based on development of the children you work with. Before you use the formula, keep the following in mind:

The younger the children, the more time they need to make choices. Think about how hard it is to program a two-year-old child and how he typically responds when you try to take control from him.

When you have calculated all of the time your children are in school and the amount of time that you allow them to have some choices, and you find you have more than the formula recommends, do not panic. The formula is the *least* you should allow, more only strengthens your program.

At the beginning of the school year, you should use the percentages from the previous age group. A kindergartner is much more like a preschool child in the first part of the school year than the confident children you may remember from the end of the previous year. After all, they have only had a summer vacation since they were in preschool.

Calculate all of the time your children are in school, not just the time with you in the classroom. For example, count the time with special teachers, lunch, bathroom breaks and playground time. To young children, all of the time in the school building is "school."

When you add the times that children are in choice activities, be sure that they are truly choice activities. A good way to look at this issue is to think of it from the children's point of view and ask yourself: "Are the children going to feel as if they have real, authentic control and choices during this time?"

Schedule Formula

3- to 4-Year-Olds
75% Choice Time
25% Teacher Directed

Kindergartners
50% Choice Time
50% Teacher Directed

1st–2nd Graders
33% Choice Time
66% Teacher Directed

3rd–4th Graders
20% Choice Time
80% Teacher Directed

Examples:
Your Schedule

Learning centers–45 min.
Table toys–25 min.
Snack time–15 min.
Story time–15 min.

Learning centers–45 min.
Library–20 min.
Math time–20 min.
Story–15 min.
Music–10 min.

Learning centers–30 min.
Journals–20 min.
Math
P.E.
Music

_____
_____
_____
_____
_____

The Class Meeting

A class meeting is an effective way to allow children to plan for their time in learning centers.

What is a class meeting? A whole class meeting where children are seated on the floor and plan for the center work they will do during work time.

How long should the class meeting last? An average time for a class meeting is fifteen minutes. Any longer is frustrating. This time should not include other types of whole group discussions. For example: Avoid discussing the helper chart, calendar, weather or collecting snack money. This time should be focused on discussing centers and all other business should be handled at another time.

What is the teacher's role during the class meeting? The teacher's role is to facilitate the meeting by directing open-ended questions to the children and to encourage an interchange of ideas between the students.

Type of Class Meeting

Regular:

Each child is seated on the floor in a circle. The teacher facilitates the meeting and allows each child an opportunity to share his plans with the others.

Planning Ladder:

A long roll of paper with the symbols of each center drawn on the paper in permanent markers. During the class meeting, the planning ladder is rolled out in the center of the circle where the children are seated. Each child, in turn, walks down the ladder, stands on the symbol of the center she plans to go to first during work time, and describes what she plans to do at that center.

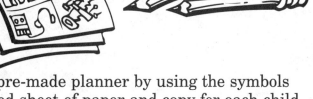

Written Plans:

For younger children, make a pre-made planner by using the symbols from each center on a duplicated sheet of paper and copy for each child. Ask the children to circle the centers they plan to work at first. The planning sheet may be stored in a pocket on the planning board described on pages 19 and 20.

Type of Class Meeting

Older children may use a blank sheet of paper or a spiral notebook for recording center work. On one side of the paper children will draw a picture and write a short description of their plans. At the end of the center time, the children can reflect on how their plans changed.

Planning Partners:

Children are divided into pairs and discuss their plans with their partners. The teacher should use this time to visit with each group and listen to their planning, facilitate any problems and encourage each child to listen and comment. Children may remain with the same partner for several weeks or change on a regular basis.

Examples of Planning Boards

Planning boards are used as visual charts during the class meeting.

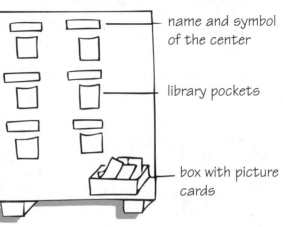

name and symbol of the center

library pockets

box with picture cards

Free-Standing Planning Board

Pizza Round Planning Chart

puzzles

art

blocks

language

clothespin with each child's name printed on in marker

pizza round covered with clear adhesive paper

symbol for each center

This concept is very portable so that the class meeting can be held in a variety of places in the room.

Small Pocket Chart

This chart will not take much space.

Tongue depressor with child's name printed on in marker

Andre

library pocket

Examples of Planning Boards

Chalk or Magnetic Board

Planning boards are used as visual charts during the class meeting.

Learning Centers

Listening

Sand Table

Science

Storage for Written Plans

This concept works best with older children who can complete written plans successfully.

Tasha
Barb
Jose
Mike
Debbie
Carlos
Mark
Carol
Kiya

Learning Centers File Box

Review Time

Giving your children choices about their work at learning centers is a critical way to improve the work children do during this time.

To strengthen the learning center time even more, a review time will allow children to debrief their plans from the class meeting and set the stage for the next day's work at learning centers.

It is human nature to need to review or culminate an activity before you move on to another.

You may realize how critical it is to review any significant activity where you have invested time and thought if you have ever had one of the following situations where no feedback was given to you:

- Have you ever written a research paper for a college course, turned it in at the last meeting of the class and received in the mail only a grade report for the class with no information about how you did on the paper or comments from the professor?

- Have you ever spent time shopping to select a gift for a friend or family member, wrapped and mailed the package and never heard if the gift was appreciated or even received?

Class Meeting, Work Time at Learning Centers, Review Cycle

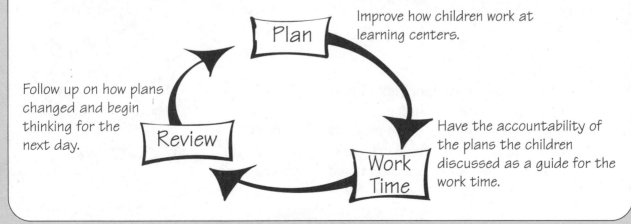

Plan — Improve how children work at learning centers.

Work Time — Have the accountability of the plans the children discussed as a guide for the work time.

Review — Follow up on how plans changed and begin thinking for the next day.

Asking Open-Ended Questions

Compare the type of questions a teacher asks in a review session to those that a lawyer asks a witness during a trial.

Lawyers ask questions they have prepared ahead of time with their clients, and as a result they know the answers they are going to get. Lawyers are also discouraged from asking questions that encourage the witness to make personal judgements. For example:

Where was the shop clerk standing?
When did you arrive at the site?

In a review session, the teacher asks questions to discover what the children have learned during the work time at learning centers. The questions are open-ended and ones that she does not know the answers to in advance. The questions are structured to help children verbalize their internal discoveries and to plant ideas for future work. For example:

Tell us about your block structure.
How did you figure that out?
What else could you do to solve the problem?
Do you have a plan for work on this another day?
What will you do to make your car work better?

Restricting the Number of Children at Centers at One Time

There are several reasons for restricting the number of children allowed to work at a center at one time. For example:

- limited table space and chairs at an Art Center
- one computer available to the classroom
- a limited number of building blocks at the Block Center

Below and on the following page are some ideas for helping make the number of children allowed at the learning center clear to your students.

A sign placed on a table at each center shows the number of children who are allowed to work at the center at any given time. On the back of the pizza round a "closed" sign can show when this center is off limits for work at this time.

Hang a sign at the entrance of a learning center that allows children to place a golf tee or clothespin on the sign when working in the center. For example, if the Writing Center allows four children, a can with four clothespins would be stored near the sign.

Restricting the Number of Children at Centers at One Time

Use hooks for name tags that show the number of children allowed at the center at any one time. When a child selects a center, he places his name tag on a hook during the time he is working in the center.

Place clothespins on the outside rim of a coffee can (or other large can). The number of clothespins available on the can indicates the number allowed in the center at any given time. When a child chooses to work in the center, she removes the clothespin from the can and places it on her collar to wear while in the center. Each can could be different for each center. Wooden clothespins can be colored with marker to match the can.

Cut paper dolls from oaktag and cover with clear adhesive or laminate. The dolls can be attached to two-sided tape and mounted to a table or shelf in the learning center. Use one doll each for the number of children allowed to use the center at any one time. This method will allow you flexibility in changing the number of children at a center as you feel necessary.

Block Center

Ben   Andre   Lisa

Troubleshooting

Here are some questions that teachers ask most frequently.

What do I do about the child who moves from center to center and never settles down for any meaningful work?

Begin by thinking about reasons why a child may be unable to choose a center and settle into working on a task. Some children forget the choices and need to review them physically by moving from area to area during the first few weeks of school. Given some time, they should settle into work and stay with a task. If time does not help, you may need to work individually with the child to help her find something that she is interested in doing. When children see you will work calmly with them to completion, they will feel more secure with the materials and the room and begin to develop the skills to stay with a task.

What do you do about a child who consistently chooses the same learning center?

The problem may be insecurity. Some young children choose the area they feel most comfortable with and are hesitant to try an unfamiliar center. Time will help the child gain the confidence to branch out with his choices. The discussions you have at review time may also help give him other ideas when he hears about the exciting work that is being done at other centers.

Arranging the Classroom for Learning Centers

When learning centers work in the classroom, it is often because there is a well-thought-out plan and design in place. No two rooms are exactly alike and each has its own special assets and problems. Using learning centers in the classroom makes the use of the space a critical issue.

To begin . . .
Think how your space in the classroom is being used currently.

Space for all of the children to be seated at work areas.
Space where a small group can gather on the floor.
Space where everyone can sit in a circle.
Space for learning centers.
Space for the teacher's desk and materials.
Space for storage of coats and children's personal materials.

Consider an average week and assign an approximate percentage of time that the areas were used. Then look at the percentage of space being used for each area. Next, look at where there are discrepencies in the space versus the usage. For example, if your group circle is taking up a fourth of the space in the room, but you only use it an hour a week, that may be an area you want to rethink.

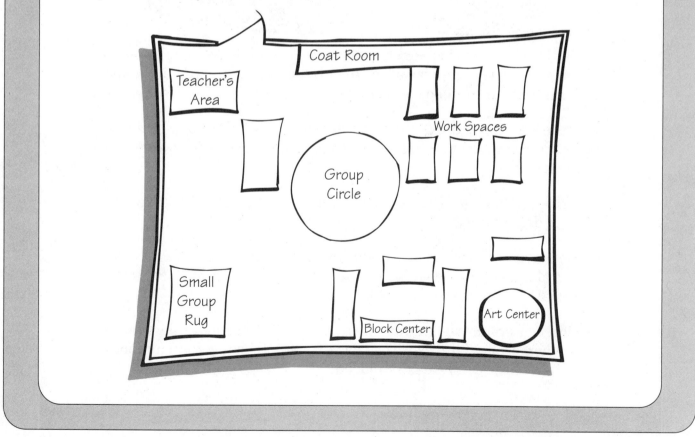

Arranging the Classroom for Learning Centers

If you plan to use learning centers for 50 percent of each day, then you should consider allocating about 50 percent of the total area to space for learning centers.

How do you do that?

Move the tables in the work space area into the learning centers. When an activity requires all of the children to be seated at tables, the children can find space to work in small groups at those tables.

Remove the tables altogether and design any whole group activities for work on the floor. Writing activities can be redesigned for work in centers.

Use the teacher's desk as a divider for a center, thus allowing it to serve a double duty.

Remove the teacher's desk altogether and clean off a shelf to store the materials that are needed most readily in the classroom. Put other materials in a teacher work area.

Design centers for the middle of the room that are more portable so that when an activity requires space for whole group instruction, the portable center can be easily moved.

Dividing the Individual Centers in the Classroom

Whenever possible, divide the individual centers in the classroom to create small, intimate spaces where it is clear to the children where they may work. Groups may be kept in more manageable sizes, and the materials will have clear spaces for storage.

The corner areas of rooms are a good place to begin to divide the centers, since the two walls act as partial divisions, but at the most you may only have two or three corners to utilize for learning centers.

Other areas may be divided by placing a shelf parallel to the wall between two centers.

In this way, the shelf offers storage for the books in the Language Center and serves as a divider between it and the Art Center.

Here are some other ways to divide the two centers.

• Use the teacher's desk as a divider. The front of a metal desk may be used in a Math Center for magnets.

• Use an easel as a divider, with one side in an Art Center for markers and the other side in a Language Center for big books.

• Turn a portable cubbie storage unit parallel to a wall, with the cubbies facing out and the back of the unit in the nearest center.

Create a center divider with a shower curtain or plastic six-pack can holders tied together with bread ties and suspended on a dowel rod from the ceiling:

This center divider works well for the Art Center. Place the easel near the shower curtain and a plastic drop cloth under it to protect the flooring.

Substitute the six-pack can holder curtain and create a space where paintings may be hung to dry.

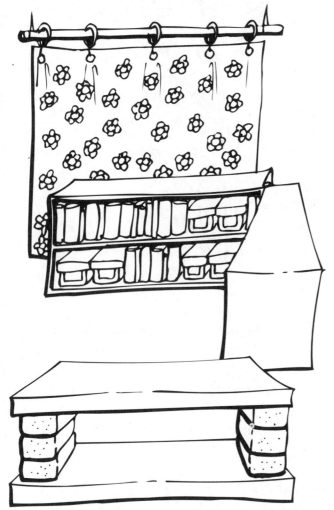

Use a hinged shelf to create a space in the center of the floor.

If this is a Math Manipulative Center, for example, the shelves may be placed on a small section of carpet and the materials stored on the two shelves. Children may take the materials off of the shelves and use them on the carpet during center time. When the center is not in use, the hinged shelves may be closed to create a counter space for snack time, for example.

Build your own custom shelves that are open for use from two centers.

This type of center divider is perfect to use between two centers where the materials may need to be shared. For example, the Block Center and Math Manipulative Center might share some of the same materials.

Making Use of Existing Furniture

Your school budget may not allow you to purchase a whole new classroom of furniture as you make the transition from a more teacher-directed classroom to a learning center format, so you will find it necessary to make the best use of existing furniture with some creative applications.

Walk around your classroom with a notepad and pencil and make an inventory of the furniture that you are currently using. Think about how you have traditionally used these pieces and how they might be used in other ways.

If you identify some things in your room that are only taking up space and will not be helpful in your learning center environment, try bartering with a colleague for a piece of furniture that might be more useful to you.

Check the hidden spaces in your school for furniture that is not being used but has great potential. For example, the boiler room often holds treasures.

You can change the uses of some furniture for more practical use in your learning centers.

Put a piece of pegboard on the back of a shelf and create additional storage space for materials stored in Ziploc™ bags and hung on hooks.

Or cover the back of a shelf with a cork board and create a display space in a center. Or cover the back with felt for a flannel board in the Language Center.

Examples of Converting Furniture for Use in Learning Centers

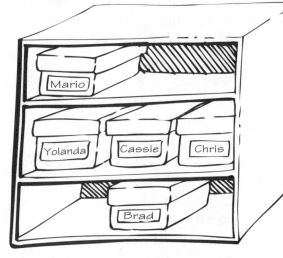

Convert a shelf to a storage compartment for the children's materials by placing tubs with each child's name on them on the shelves.

Create a Listening Center by converting the lower shelf of the teacher's closet to a quiet place for a few children to listen to tapes. Place a tape recorder on the bottom shelf. Choose a few favorite books and tapes or music for children to select on the shelf beside the tape recorder. When center time is over, close the door to the closet.

Add additional table space in a learning center by placing a sheet of plyboard on the top of two students' desks. Cover the board by painting it with a glossy enamel paint, clear self-adhesive paper or oil cloth, depending on the type of use you have in mind.

Labeling Learning Centers

A clear system for labeling learning centers will support your management system and help the children connect the name of the center in visual format with the written language.

Signs for the centers should be placed at the eye level of children. Signs that are hung from the ceiling, need to be dropped low enough for the children to see and use them. Signs may also be placed on a table or shelf in the center.

If you will be using a management system that allows children to choose their first center in a class meeting format (see Chapter 2, page 16) the signs that are used at the center need to match the visual placed on the planning board.

The key thing to consider in designing center signs is that the visuals must be clear to the children.

Which of these signs would be most appropriate for an Art Center?

The paint pallet may remind adults who have had experience with artists using the pallet for mixing colors. But for young children, most of whom would not have had an actual experience with a pallet, this would not be the best choice.

If your students will be painting on an easel, this would make a clear sign for the Art Center.

Draw the signs on white with clear black lines or copy them from another source. Use typing correction fluid to white out any parts you want to eliminate. Use a copy machine to enlarge the pictures if necessary.

Examples of Signs for Labeling Learning Centers

Book Center

Listening Center

Art Center

Woodworking Center

Block Center

Manipulative Center

Dramatic Play Center

Labeling Materials in the Learning Centers

When the materials that are available in the learning centers are clearly labeled in a way that makes sense to the children, several benefits result. First, the materials themselves become a method for teaching the printed form of the words. Studies have shown that when children see the printed word and a visual along with the actual materials, they will be able to identify the word alone in print without ever having been "taught" it with flash cards or other isolating methods. The second benefit to labeling materials comes at the end of the work time–cleanup time. Children are more likely to be able to put the materials away when the containers and their spaces are clearly marked.

The key to an effective labeling system for materials is that it makes sense to the people who must use it, the children.

Since young children learn things in a visual way, the labeling system must be visual.

Match the materials (in this case, unifix cubes)

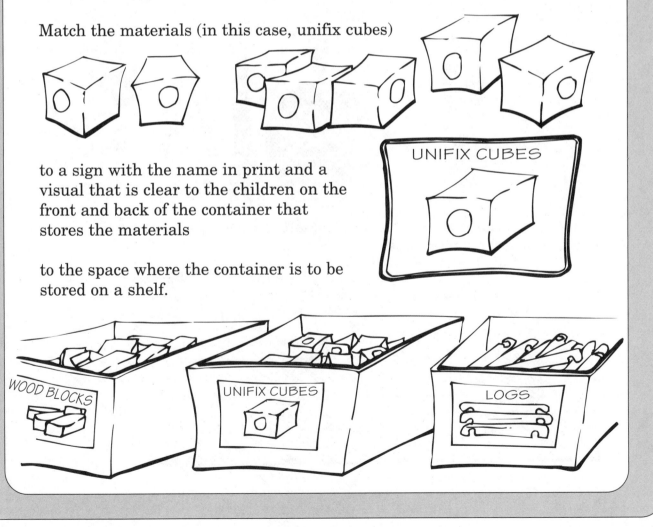

to a sign with the name in print and a visual that is clear to the children on the front and back of the container that stores the materials

to the space where the container is to be stored on a shelf.

Examples of Labeling Materials in Learning Centers

Organize unit blocks on shelves by drawing an outline of each different shape on black paper. Cut out the outline and attach to a shelf with clear self-adhesive paper where the blocks of that shape will be stored. At cleanup time the blocks are returned to the shelf by matching the shapes.

Draw an outline of materials that can be hung on pegboard on adhesive paper, cut out and apply to the pegboard at the space where the materials will be hung. Place a hook above the outline. Hang pots, pans, utensils and cups from the Dramatic Play Center or funnels from the Sand and Water Center in this method.

Place books and tapes in a clear Ziploc™ bag. Punch a hole in the top of the bag and hang on pegboard in the Listening Center.

Organize boxes that tend to look alike on a shelf with a matching color of self-adhesive paper.

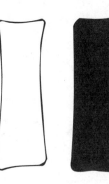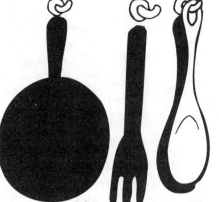

This method may be used for puzzles, lotto games, board games and trays of matching materials.

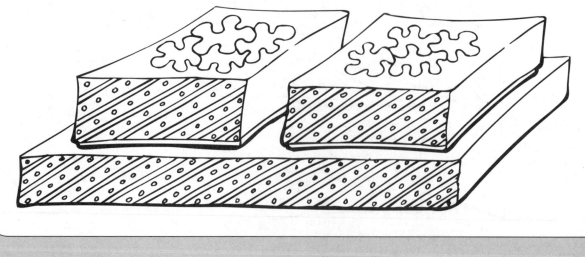

Cleanup Time

Cleanup time is a hectic time in the schedule for all early childhood class-rooms, and learning centers can provide even more stress. You can create a more managable system for cleanup time by implementing the organizational suggestions given earlier in this chapter. When the materials are clearly labeled for children in a way that makes sense to them, the cleanup time is easier for them and less stressful for you.

The following are some additional tips, used by veteran learning center teachers for cleanup time:

- Give the children a calm warning a few minutes before you intend to start the cleanup time. They will probably not start automatically with the warning, but they will not be as shocked when it is time to begin in earnest.

- Areas that take more time to clean up may need to start ahead of the others. For example, the Block Center may need to begin a few minutes before the others to quietly put away all of the materials that they have taken off of shelves.

- Encourage everyone to pick up even if it is "not their mess" as they will often complain. Calmly say, "We just all help to pick up everything." Young children often don't remember that they were at the Puzzle Center earlier in the work time and forgot to put their puzzle away.

- Be sure that any adult helpers that are in the room are helping with the cleanup time as much as the children–in addition to providing calm reassurance and advice.

- Allow children who want to go to another area to clean up rather than the center that they were working in, to do that. As long as they are contributing to the cleanup efforts, it may be a way for them to participate in a center that they did not work in during the session.

- Notice how many times the word *calm* is used or inferred. That is the key; **stay calm**.

Examples of Room Arrangements with Learning Centers and Desks

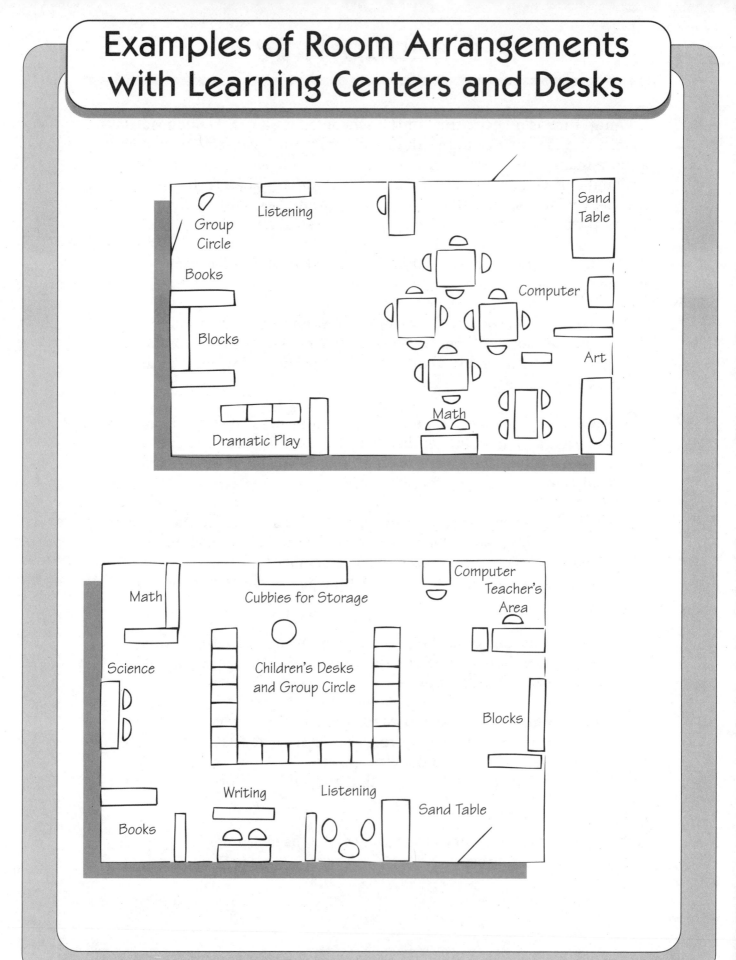

Examples of Classrooms with Tables Used in Learning Centers

In this floor plan the students sit on the floor for group time (class meeting, helper chart, story reading, etc.) and use the tables in the centers for any whole group project that requires writing space for every child. During work time, the tables are used as part of the centers, thus freeing floor space for more centers and eliminating the need for space for individual student desks.

On the preceding page are tools for you to plan your room arrangement. Graph paper will help you match the floor space for your room. On page 38 are samples of commonly found furniture that you can copy, cut out and place on the grid paper. Begin by drawing in doors, windows and permanent furniture (for example, a sink area or teacher's closet). Try a variety of arrangements to see what seems to work well for ease of movement.

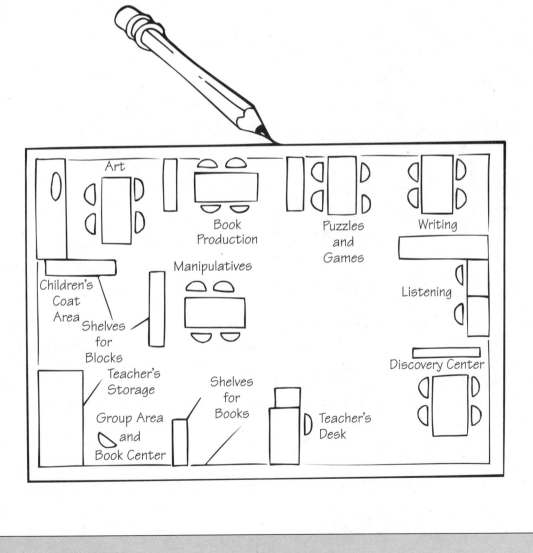

Questions Teachers Ask Most Frequently

Where do I begin to label my learning center materials?

Begin with the area that is the most difficult for your children to clean up. Most likely, the trouble is the way the materials are organized.

What do I do with my teaching materials?

If the area you have set aside for your teacher materials (including desk, file, computer, etc.) takes up a significant amount of space compared with the area for learning centers, you may need to think about alternative storage. Move materials that you use frequently, but not daily, to a higher shelf and free lower shelves for learning center materials. Move seldom-used materials to a closet or a teacher storage room. Place your desk in an out-of-the-way space, or consider trading your large desk for a smaller one. You can even remove your teacher desk and place frequently used materials in a basket that can easily be transported to any space you choose to work.

Chapter 4
The Art Center

The Art Center

The Art Center is designed to be a busy production center. Ideally, it should have a water source and tile floor. The storage space should allow children to find a variety of materials easily accessable, in labeled tubs. Materials such as crayons and scissors are organized so that the children can use and replace them.

The Art Center

Justification for the Art Center

Mount a sign in the Art Center at an adult's eye level that states why you have made the educational decision to have an Art Center in your classroom.

The Art Center is a place where children can explore a variety of interesting materials. Young children show us what they know through their artwork. They learn by using the senses and the Art Center provides a multisensory experience for them. Our Art Center is available for daily work that children plan and implement, choosing from materials such as paints, crayons, clay, colored pencils and odds and ends we find in everyday settings.

Objectives That May Be Developed in Activities

- Creativity is enhanced when children have a variety of interesting materials to explore.
- The Art Center is a representational center, meaning that through their artistic interpretations, the children show you what they are interested in learning about.
- New sensory experiences are available with a wide variety of art supplies.
- Children are making plans, solving problems and learning to negotiate during the development of an art project.

The Art Center

The Art Center Materials

A variety of types of papers should be readily available to the children in the Art Center. Paper should be stored flat where the types and colors are easy to identify. Include construction paper, wrapping paper, foil, card stock and waxed paper.

Store art supplies in sturdy plastic containers with lids that the children can remove and replace with ease. Mark the outside of the container with the name and a visual of the contents. Types of supplies should include crayons, colored pencils, pastel colors, markers, scissors, plastic knives, a variety of lids for making circles, stencils and pencils.

Clay, play dough and other types of texture mixtures should be stored in airtight containers. Small individual amounts can be kept in butter tubs. Larger amounts can be stored in a coffee can, a Ziploc™ bag or a kitchen canister.

The Art Center

The Art Center Materials

Paints should be stored in airtight containers. Add soap flakes to pre-mixed paints to keep them fresh longer. Keep a large coffee can with clean water near the painting area for washing brushes. Brushes should be stored with the brush end up to dry thoroughly and not damage the bristles.

Store other materials in a plastic tub, shoe box or plastic crate on a shelf with a sign telling the name and a picture of the materials stored. Other materials that may accumulate in the center during the year include the following:

cotton balls
leather scraps
yarn
bread ties
bows
ribbon scraps
thread
old buttons
plastic scraps
Styrofoam™
old greeting cards
hole punch dots
magazines
workbook pictures
slides, etc.

As the children develop their art, add other tools to the Art Center to vary the types of work that they are able to do.

Tasks in the Art Center

Tasks are added to the basic materials in a learning center to enhance the experience for the children. Begin the Art Center with the basic materials and then add new tasks, one at a time. These tasks are designed to be child-directed. The titles tell you the following:

Task: The name of the new collection of materials to be added to the center.

Goal: One possible skill, knowledge or disposition children may develop as a result of this experience.

Materials: Materials you will need to collect for this task.

Preparations: A description of the preparations you will need to make before you present the task into the learning center.

Notes: Follow-up or additional ideas of things children may do as a result of this experience. For example:

Markers at the Easel

Goal: Children may explore using markers on an upright surface.

Materials:

a child-size easel
nontoxic markers in a variety of colors
art paper or newsprint

Preparations: Replace the traditional tempera paint with markers.

Notes: To help with clean-up at the easel, cut a section of Styrofoam™ to fit the tray of the easel. Place the marker caps into the Styrofoam™. Children can remove the marker, but leave the cap in place so that they will be more likely to replace the cap on the marker.

Still Life Painting

Goal: Children will experience the skills necessary to paint a representational picture.

Materials:

dry tempera paint
muffin tin
small brushes
container for water
art paper
"still life" object

Preparations: Place the still life object at a table in the Art Center. Choose colors of the dry tempera paint that will be useful for the children to use in creating the painting. Put a small amount of each color in the different sections of the muffin tin. Place a few small brushes in the container with water. Demonstrate how to mix a small amount of water into the paint to create different intensities of colors.

Notes: Add a small board to the task for mixing colors. Substitute brushes with other tools for painting. For example: cotton swabs, feathers or a fern. Add watercolor paints for a softer look to the paintings.

Greeting Card Tubs

Goal: To give children a collection of materials that will encourage them to make greeting cards for others.

Materials:

plastic tub with lid
construction paper
yarn
tissue paper
honeycomb paper
crayons
pipe cleaners
various odds and ends

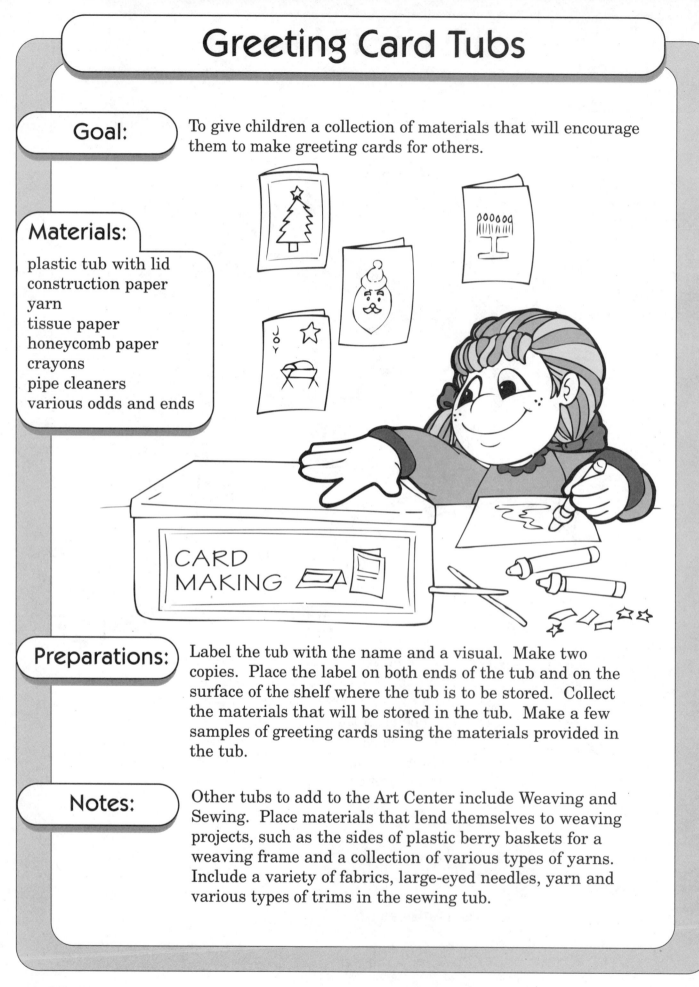

Preparations: Label the tub with the name and a visual. Make two copies. Place the label on both ends of the tub and on the surface of the shelf where the tub is to be stored. Collect the materials that will be stored in the tub. Make a few samples of greeting cards using the materials provided in the tub.

Notes: Other tubs to add to the Art Center include Weaving and Sewing. Place materials that lend themselves to weaving projects, such as the sides of plastic berry baskets for a weaving frame and a collection of various types of yarns. Include a variety of fabrics, large-eyed needles, yarn and various types of trims in the sewing tub.

Outdoor Collage

Goal: An opportunity for children to explore collage work using materials gathered from nature.

Materials:

pizza round
white glue
variety of nature
    materials including
    pinecones, leaves,
    sweet gum balls,
    sticks, seashells
    and pieces from
    evergreen trees
set of small boxes

SHELLS

PINECONES AND EVERGREENS

LEAVES

Preparations: Gather the nature materials in a set of small boxes. Label each box with the name and a visual. Make a sample collage for display in the Art Center. Assist the children in choosing a pizza round as the surface for their collage. Use white glue to attach the materials onto the surface.

Notes: The finished products may become wreaths to hang by gluing a paper clip near the top of the back of the pizza round.

The Mural Station

Goal: An opportunity for children to explore painting on a large surface.

Materials:

newsprint
tempera paint
large brushes
plastic drop cloth
water container

Preparations: Tape a large sheet of newsprint on a wall. Place a plastic drop cloth on the floor underneath the newsprint. Mix a variety of colors of paint for the children to use for their paintings. You may help the children get started with their mural by painting a basic outline of a tree or a house for them to add details.

Notes: Add collage materials to the mural station and glue. Allow the children to explore adding dimension to their murals. Create murals that follow a current theme or topic. For example: If you are working on a theme of transportation, encourage children to paint a mural of an airport, bus depot or train station.

Chapter 5
The Block Center

The Block Center

The Block Center is a construction area designed for movement and large materials. It should have a well-defined space with open-style bookcases for storage and a low-nap carpet on the floor. This will be an active area of the classroom and would ideally be located out of the traffic flow.

The Block Center

Mount a sign in the Block Center at an adult's eye level that states why you have made the educational decision to have a Block Center in your classroom.

The Block Center is an area that provides children with interesting construction materials for designing and building. Because of its arrangement, this center allows small groups of children to share materials, work together to make designs and work out problems they encounter with their projects. Children learn about shapes, size, measurement, distance and many building skills. But one of the most important skills that will be developed when children are in the Block Center is working in collaboration with others.

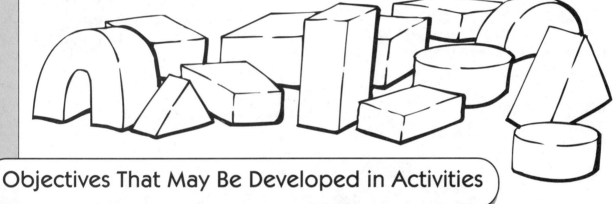

Objectives That May Be Developed in Activities

- Work in the Block Center simulates real work for the child in organizing a project design and implementing it with the materials available.
- Blocks develop a variety of logical/mathematical thinking including classification, measurement, fractions and order.
- Patterning, balance and symmetry are achieved with work in the Block Center.
- The work with the materials in the Block Center allows exploration in stability, balance and cause and effect.
- Children's building structures represent what they know about real structures they have seen and studied.

The Block Center

The Block Center Materials

The basic material necessary for an effective Block Center is a set of unit blocks. To accommodate a group of three to six children in a Block Center, a fourth of the set of unit blocks is adequate. Typically, about 160 blocks of a variety of shapes are included in a fourth of the set of unit blocks.

Accessory pieces will enhance the work at the Block Center. Trucks, road signs and environmental pieces help make the structures more realistic for children. They should be added to the Block Center where they are easily accessible.

People and animal pieces also enhance the work that children can do when working in the Block Center.

The Block Center

The Block Center Materials

Other building materials added to the Block Center will increase the creativity of the work.

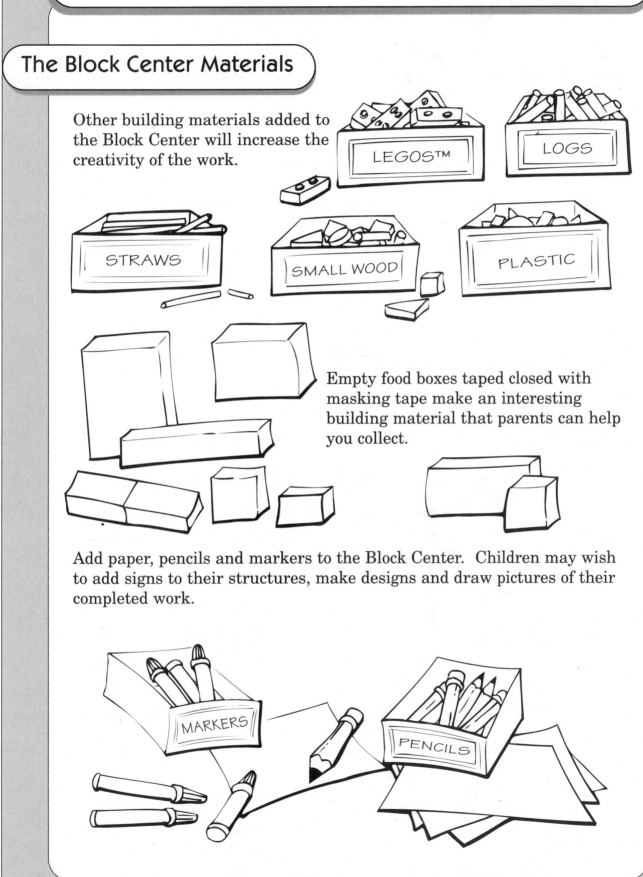

Empty food boxes taped closed with masking tape make an interesting building material that parents can help you collect.

Add paper, pencils and markers to the Block Center. Children may wish to add signs to their structures, make designs and draw pictures of their completed work.

Tasks in the Block Center

Tasks are added to the basic materials in a learning center to enhance the experience for the children. Begin the Block Center with the basic materials and then add new tasks, one at a time. These tasks are designed to be child-directed. The titles tell you the following:

Task: The name of the new collection of materials to be added to the center.

Goal: One possible skill, knowledge or disposition children may develop as a result of this experience.

Materials: Materials you will need to collect for this task.

Preparations: A description of the preparations you will need to make before you present the task into the learning center.

Notes: Follow-up or additional ideas of things children may do as a result of this experience. For example:

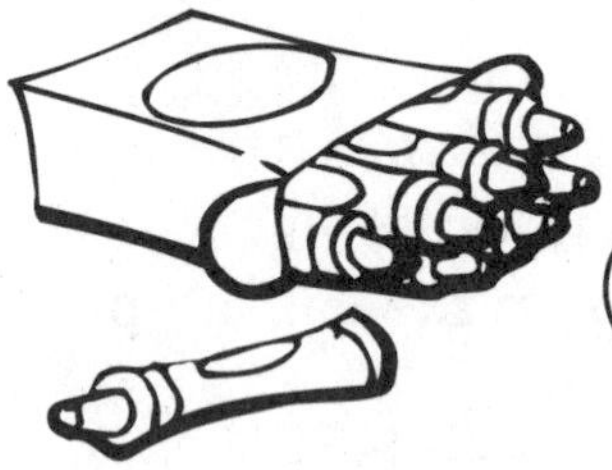

Building Map

Goal: To allow children to make their own maps for their building structures.

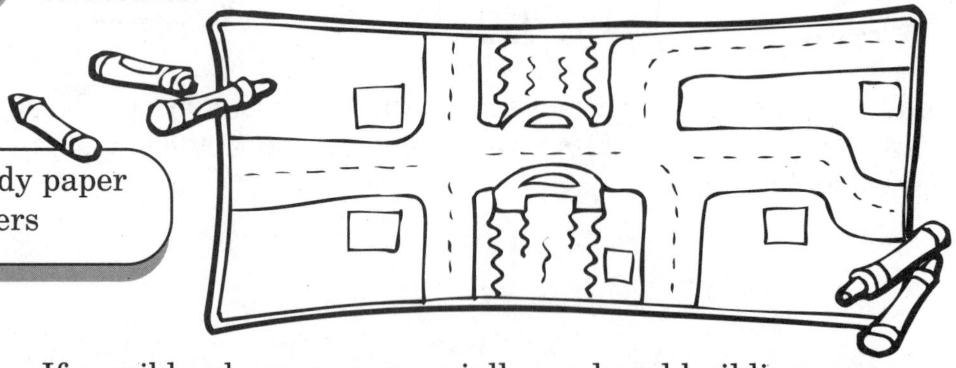

Materials:

large sheet of sturdy paper
crayons and markers

Preparations: If possible, share a commercially produced building map with the children to give them the idea for making their own. Place the materials in the Block Center and suggest that the children may work in small groups to make maps for their buildings.

Notes: Add road signs to the building map.

Outdoor Environments

Goal: To allow children to add real materials from nature to their building structures.

Materials:

tub with lid
sticks
leaves
pinecones
sweet gum balls
clay

Preparations: You may wish to let the children help in collecting materials by taking a nature walk. Gather the materials into the tub. Label the tub with a name and visual. Children can use the materials to make trees, shrubs and ground cover to enhance their building structures.

Notes: Combine this task with the Building Map task on page 56.

People-Making Kit

Goal: To develop the interest in children to add people to their building structures.

Materials:

tub with lid
wooden clothespins
various fabrics
wide-eyed needles
yarn and thread
markers

Preparations: Place a large sheet of paper, markers and other materials in the center for children to make a floor map.

Notes: Add people from other building sets to the Block Center to add interest to the building structures.

Hard Hats

Goal: Props such as hard hats will add the feeling that children are representing the role of a builder.

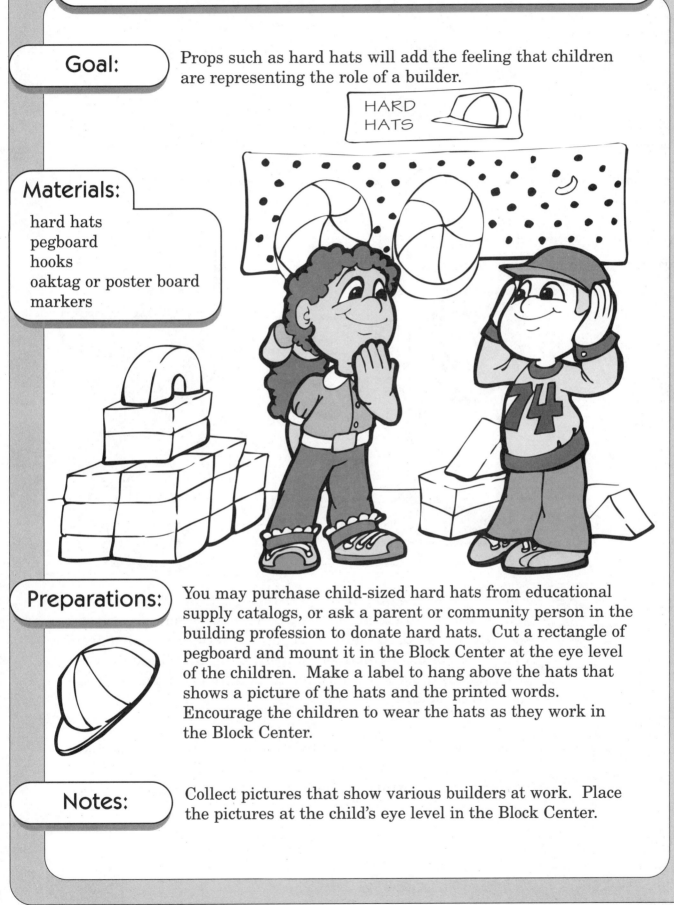

Materials:

hard hats
pegboard
hooks
oaktag or poster board
markers

Preparations: You may purchase child-sized hard hats from educational supply catalogs, or ask a parent or community person in the building profession to donate hard hats. Cut a rectangle of pegboard and mount it in the Block Center at the eye level of the children. Make a label to hang above the hats that shows a picture of the hats and the printed words. Encourage the children to wear the hats as they work in the Block Center.

Notes: Collect pictures that show various builders at work. Place the pictures at the child's eye level in the Block Center.

Appliance Box Buildings

Goal: To allow children to explore possibilities of building with large cardboard boxes.

Materials:

large appliance boxes
tempera paint
paintbrushes
plastic drop cloth or old newspapers

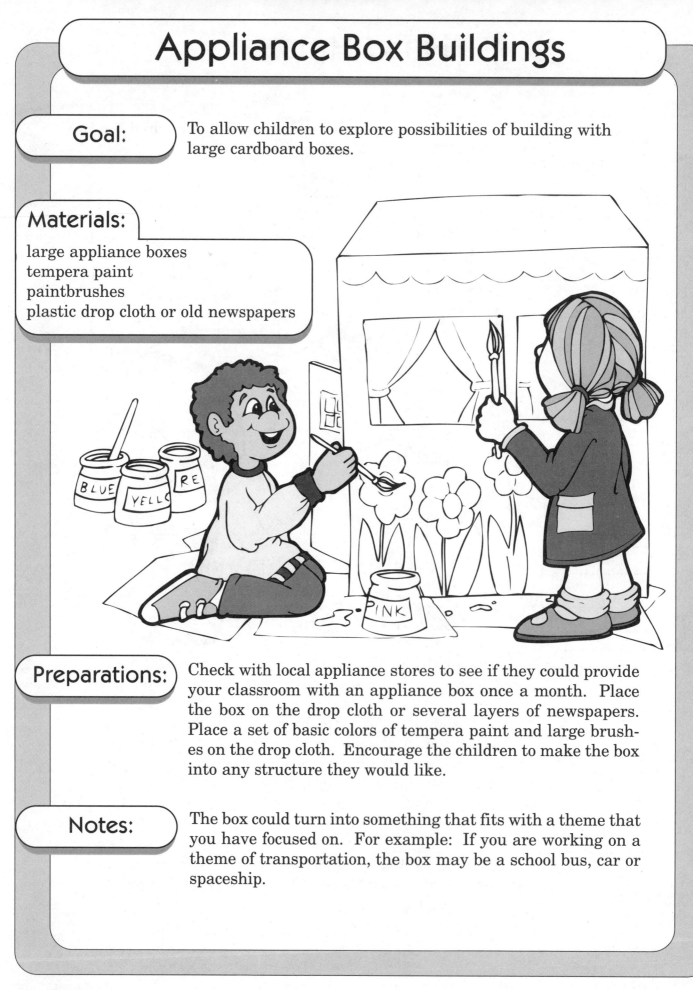

Preparations: Check with local appliance stores to see if they could provide your classroom with an appliance box once a month. Place the box on the drop cloth or several layers of newspapers. Place a set of basic colors of tempera paint and large brushes on the drop cloth. Encourage the children to make the box into any structure they would like.

Notes: The box could turn into something that fits with a theme that you have focused on. For example: If you are working on a theme of transportation, the box may be a school bus, car or spaceship.

Class Trip Poster

Goal: To document the buildings children encounter on a class field trip that they may wish to reproduce with the materials in the Block Center.

Materials:
camera and film
poster board
markers
glue

THE ZOO

Our class trip to the zoo.   An elephant   The lions

The bird cage.   Tiger   ake

WOOD BLOCKS

Preparations: Take a camera with you on a field trip, and take pictures of various buildings that the children encounter. Include small groups of the children in the pictures whenever possible. Develop the film and make a poster that clearly shows the events of the field trip with captions printed with markers. Mount the poster in the Block Center at the children's eye level. You will find that the children refer to the poster and use the information for making their own structures.

Notes: Take pictures of buildings in the neighborhood that are familiar to the children and include them in the Block Center for reference in building. The buildings need not be outstanding architecture but rather familiar places that the children encounter on a regular basis. For example, a church, the school, a grocery store or convenience store.

Our Block Structures

Goal: To document the buildings for children and to preserve the structures after they have been taken down.

Materials:

scrapbook or photo album
camera and film
paper and pencil

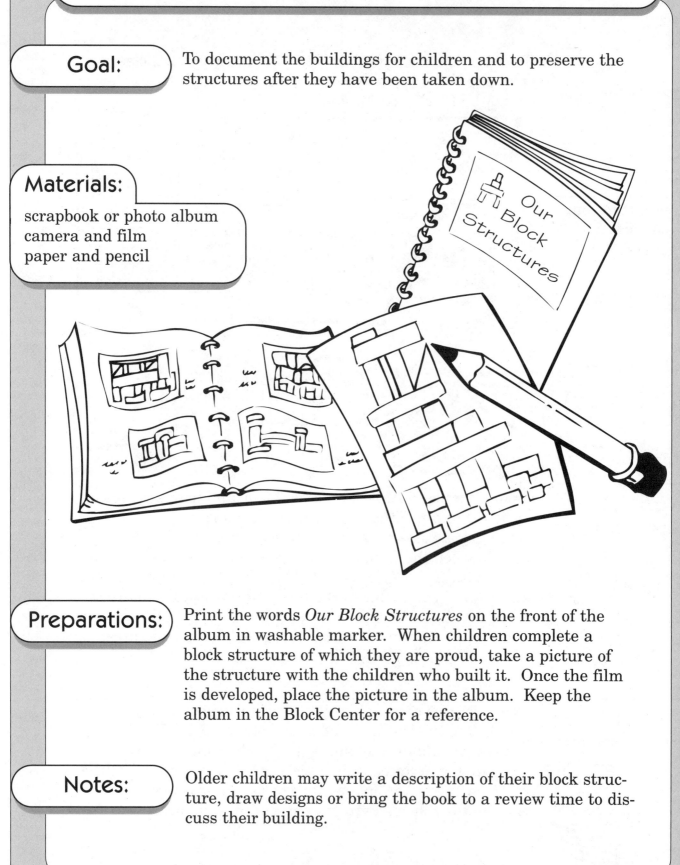

Preparations: Print the words *Our Block Structures* on the front of the album in washable marker. When children complete a block structure of which they are proud, take a picture of the structure with the children who built it. Once the film is developed, place the picture in the album. Keep the album in the Block Center for a reference.

Notes: Older children may write a description of their block structure, draw designs or bring the book to a review time to discuss their building.

The Book Center

The Book Center is designed to be a comfortable space where children relax, enjoy and explore books. Although this center may be best placed in a quiet area of the classroom, it is not always an area that is silent. When children gather to look and share books, they will talk and that is one of the objectives of this center. This is a gathering space for the children and their favorite books.

The Book Center

Justification for the Book Center

Mount a sign in the Book Center at an adult's eye level that states why you have made the educational decision to have a Book Center in your classroom.

The Book Center creates a comfortable space for children to explore and enjoy good books. Since we know that young children need to hear the same books over and over again in order to begin the process of understanding printed language, this center is designed for that purpose. Favorite books are displayed with cozy space for reading alone or with a friend. In the early stages of reading, young children will "pretend" read. Next they will sound as if they are "reading." Both of these stages support the development of the skill of decoding words. In the Book Center we will have an opportunity to observe the children as they transition through the stages and develop into competent, confident readers.

Objectives That May Be Developed in Activities

- Children will have an opportunity to hold and read a book that was shared in a whole group setting during story time.
- The emergent reading stages will be observed in an informal setting.
- Children can interact with each other as they look through books and discuss ideas.
- A comfortable setting will help establish reading books as an enjoyable, calming activity.

The Book Center

The Book Center Materials

Children's books should be displayed in a way that allows them to be viewed from the front. Choose books that have been recently read to the children. Do not try to store hundreds of books in the Book Center. Only the most recent favorites should be displayed and rotated in and out of this center.

After you have used a big book with a small group of children or the entire class, place it in the Book Center where children can read it again. Other favorite big books may be stored in this area.

Place a chart stand with large lined or unlined chart paper and markers in the Book Center. Encourage children to write their own stories.

Some soft pillows and a bean-bag chair make the Book Center a comfortable place to enjoy a good book.

Tasks in the Book Center

Tasks are added to the basic materials in a learning center to enhance the experience for the children. Begin the Book Center with the basic materials and then add new tasks, one at a time. These tasks are designed to be child-directed. The titles tell you the following:

Task: The name of the new collection of materials to be added to the center.

Goal: One possible skill, knowledge or disposition children may develop as a result of this experience.

Materials: Materials you will need to collect for this task.

Preparations: A description of the preparations you will need to make before you present the task into the learning center.

Notes: Follow-up or additional ideas of things children may do as a result of this experience. For example:

Computers in the Book Center

Goal: To allow children to explore the writing process with a computer.

Materials:

chart stand and paper
markers
computer with word
  processing program
printer

Preparations: Choose a topic that is interesting to children. Write a story on chart paper with a small group or the whole class. For example: a field trip, a letter to a classmate or a poem they enjoy. Place the chart stand in the Book Center next to the computer. Children may copy the story by using the word processing program and print a copy to take home.

Notes: You may wish to encourage the children to work in pairs at the computer.

Class Books

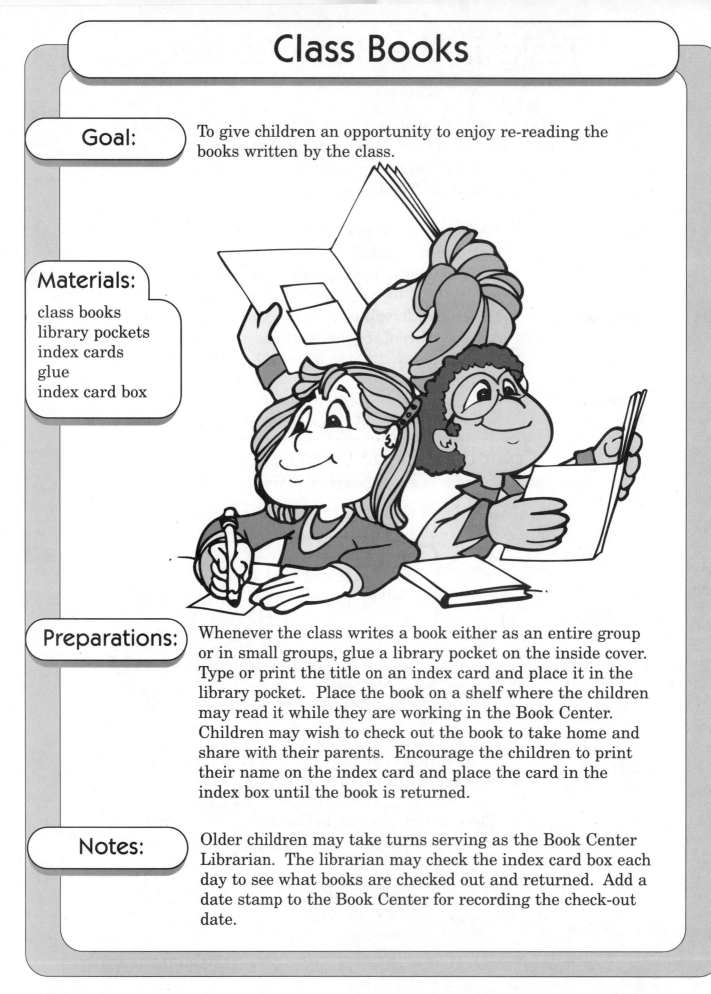

Goal: To give children an opportunity to enjoy re-reading the books written by the class.

Materials:

class books
library pockets
index cards
glue
index card box

Preparations: Whenever the class writes a book either as an entire group or in small groups, glue a library pocket on the inside cover. Type or print the title on an index card and place it in the library pocket. Place the book on a shelf where the children may read it while they are working in the Book Center. Children may wish to check out the book to take home and share with their parents. Encourage the children to print their name on the index card and place the card in the index box until the book is returned.

Notes: Older children may take turns serving as the Book Center Librarian. The librarian may check the index card box each day to see what books are checked out and returned. Add a date stamp to the Book Center for recording the check-out date.

Pocket Charts

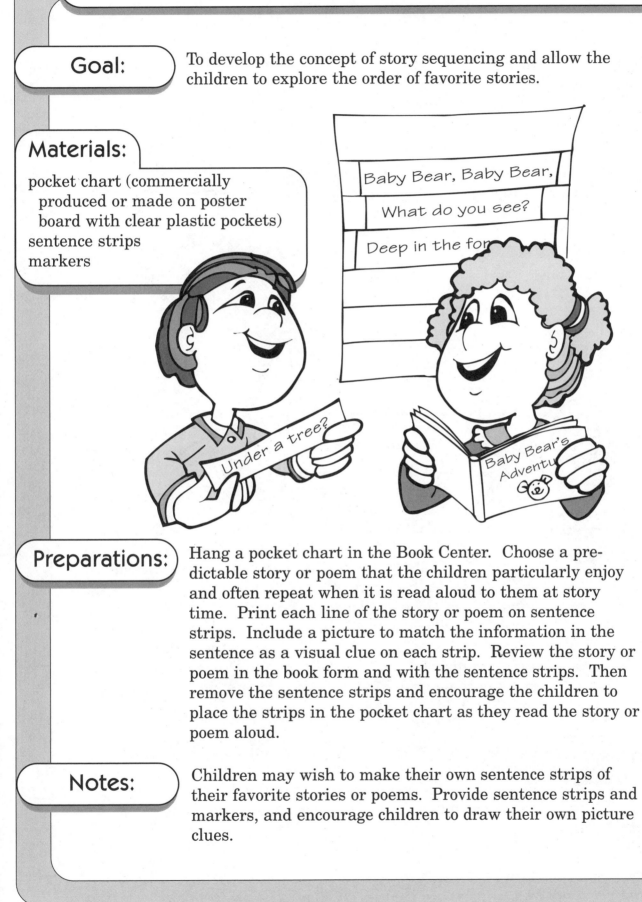

Goal: To develop the concept of story sequencing and allow the children to explore the order of favorite stories.

Materials:

pocket chart (commercially produced or made on poster board with clear plastic pockets)
sentence strips
markers

Baby Bear, Baby Bear,

What do you see?

Deep in the for

Under a tree?

Baby Bear's Adventu

Preparations: Hang a pocket chart in the Book Center. Choose a predictable story or poem that the children particularly enjoy and often repeat when it is read aloud to them at story time. Print each line of the story or poem on sentence strips. Include a picture to match the information in the sentence as a visual clue on each strip. Review the story or poem in the book form and with the sentence strips. Then remove the sentence strips and encourage the children to place the strips in the pocket chart as they read the story or poem aloud.

Notes: Children may wish to make their own sentence strips of their favorite stories or poems. Provide sentence strips and markers, and encourage children to draw their own picture clues.

Book-Making Station

Goal: To make materials available for children to create their own books.

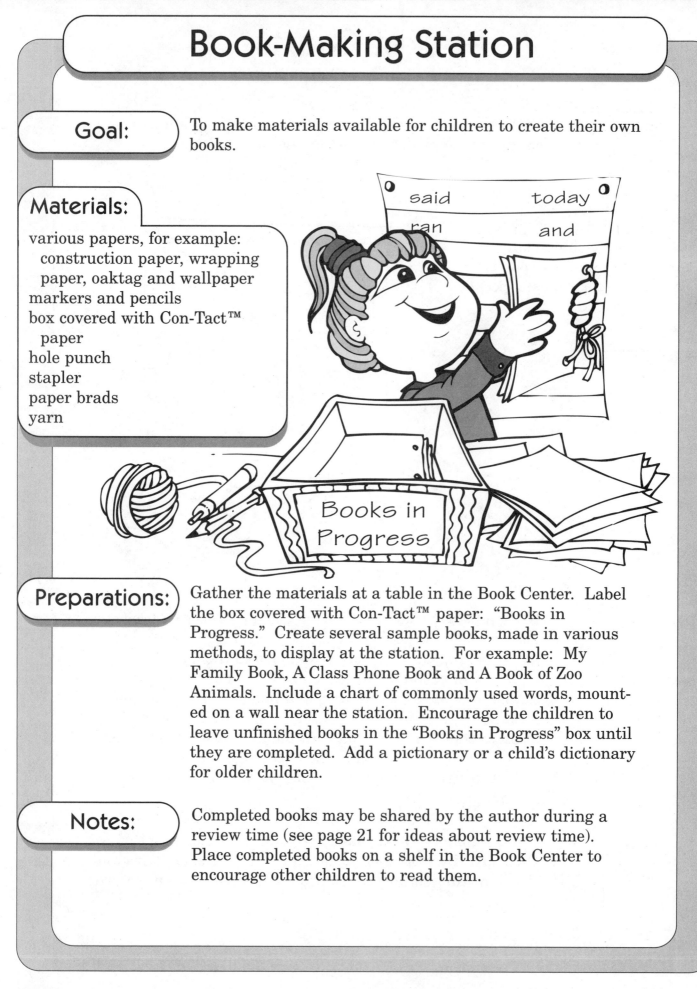

Materials:

various papers, for example:
  construction paper, wrapping
  paper, oaktag and wallpaper
markers and pencils
box covered with Con-Tact™
  paper
hole punch
stapler
paper brads
yarn

Preparations: Gather the materials at a table in the Book Center. Label the box covered with Con-Tact™ paper: "Books in Progress." Create several sample books, made in various methods, to display at the station. For example: My Family Book, A Class Phone Book and A Book of Zoo Animals. Include a chart of commonly used words, mounted on a wall near the station. Encourage the children to leave unfinished books in the "Books in Progress" box until they are completed. Add a pictionary or a child's dictionary for older children.

Notes: Completed books may be shared by the author during a review time (see page 21 for ideas about review time). Place completed books on a shelf in the Book Center to encourage other children to read them.

Book Graph

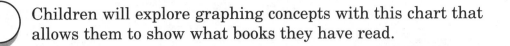

Goal: Children will explore graphing concepts with this chart that allows them to show what books they have read.

Materials:

poster board
peel-off dots
construction paper
markers
glue

Preparations: Print the title of the chart on the top of the poster board as shown in the diagram. Make miniatures of some of the children's favorite books from construction paper and glue them on the left side of the chart. Draw a vertical line with a marker to set apart the book covers. Place a box with peel-off dots on the wall next to the chart. Show the chart to the children and discuss some of the books. Children can record what books they have read by placing a dot on the chart next to the book cover. Use the chart in subsequent discussions about the most popular books and other information gained from reviewing the graph.

Notes: Allow older children to make their own book covers and survey friends in other classrooms. Display the graphs in the Book Center with the name and age of the children surveyed. For example: Favorite Books in Mrs. Scott's 2nd Grade Room.

Book Categories

Goal:

To help children explore the various categories of books and to promote organizational skills.

Materials:

plastic tubs
oaktag
markers
glue

Preparations:

Organize the books in the Book Center in plastic tubs by category. Make a label for each tub by printing the name of the category and a visual that will reinforce the category. For example: On a tub of books about dinosaurs, print the name and draw or glue a picture of a dinosaur. Place a label on the front and back of each end of the tub and on the shelf where the tub should be replaced. (For an explanation about the procedure of labeling materials for young children see page 35.) Place the tubs on a low shelf, easily accessable to the children.

Notes:

Organize the books according to the various themes you plan to explore throughout the year. Introduce each new tub into the Book Center as the theme begins. Leave old tubs on the shelf since children will often look for old favorites and enjoy reading them over and over again.

Our Favorite Books Book

Goal: To record the books children enjoy reading and listening to and to give them the opportunity to see the favorites of other classmates.

Materials:
scrapbook or photo album
camera and film
glue
paper and pencil

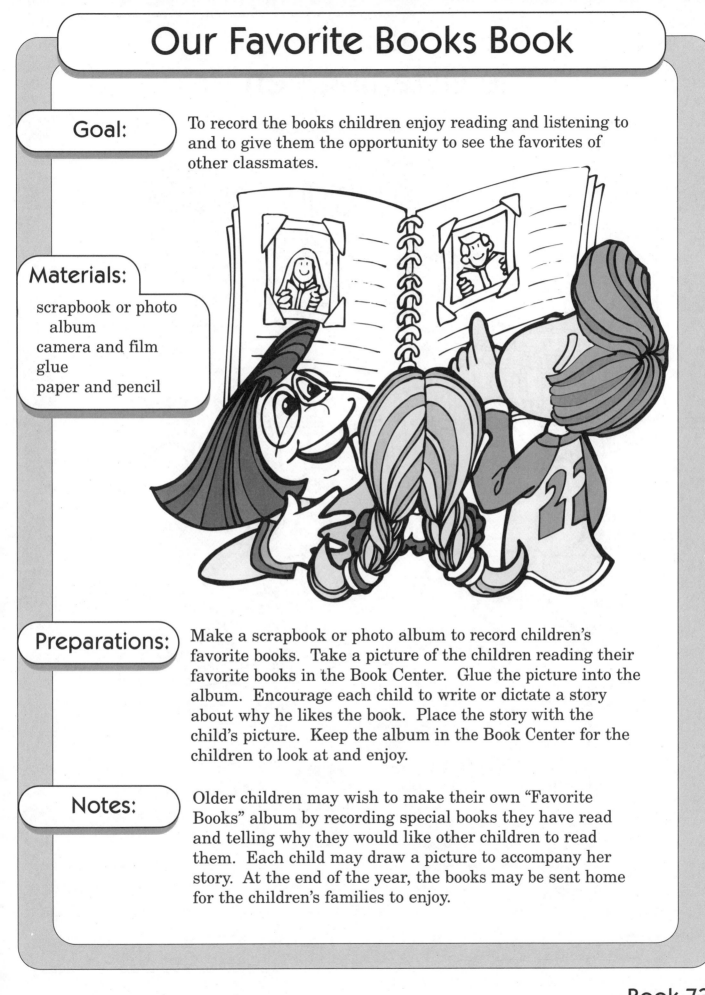

Preparations: Make a scrapbook or photo album to record children's favorite books. Take a picture of the children reading their favorite books in the Book Center. Glue the picture into the album. Encourage each child to write or dictate a story about why he likes the book. Place the story with the child's picture. Keep the album in the Book Center for the children to look at and enjoy.

Notes: Older children may wish to make their own "Favorite Books" album by recording special books they have read and telling why they would like other children to read them. Each child may draw a picture to accompany her story. At the end of the year, the books may be sent home for the children's families to enjoy.

The Listening Center

Children will gather in the Listening Center to hear books, stories and other recordings on tape. This center may not require a very large space, but it will need access to an electric outlet. You may incorporate this area next to or near the Book Center, since the work is very similar.

The Listening Center

Justification for the Listening Center

Mount a sign in the Listening Center at an adult's eye level that states why you have made the educational decision to have a Listening Center in your classroom.

Young children love to have good books and stories read to them. We know that reading aloud to children has much benefit for them emotionally as it contributes to their language development. The Listening Center is a place in your classroom devoted to providing children with a place to hear their favorite books read to them as they follow along on the printed page.

Objectives That May Be Developed in Activities

- Children will be able to hear a story while they follow the printed version in the book, thus reinforcing the concept of the language being both oral and written.

- Children will have the opportunities to hear their favorite stories, books and other types of reading repeated many times—which strengthens the connection to the printed word.

- The center may be equipped for children to make their own recordings of favorite books and oral stories.

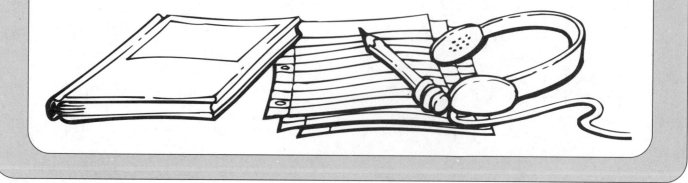

The Listening Center

The Listening Center Materials

The key piece of equipment in the Listening Center is a reliable tape recorder, preferably one that is appropriate for children to use. Check to see that it will allow you to plug in headphones, either directly to the recorder or to a headphone jack.

Storage of the tapes and books in the Listening Center is important to the success of this center. In the method shown, copies of the books and the cassette tape are placed in a Ziploc™ bag. Punch a hole in the top of the Ziploc™ bag above the locking strip. Store the books on a pegboard divider for easy access by the children. To help the children return the books and tapes to the bag, place a peel-off dot of a matching color on each book, the tape and the bag. Choose a different color for each book.

Children may be seated around a table or on a stool on the floor.

Tasks in the Listening Center

Tasks are added to the basic materials in a learning center to enhance the experience for the children. Begin the Listening Center with the basic materials and then add new tasks, one at a time. These tasks are designed to be child-directed. The titles tell you the following:

Task: The name of the new collection of materials to be added to the center.

Goal: One possible skill, knowledge or disposition children may develop as a result of this experience.

Materials: Materials you will need to collect for this task.

Preparations: A description of the preparations you will need to make before you present the task into the learning center.

Notes: Follow-up or additional ideas of things children may do as a result of this experience. For example:

Recording Favorite Books

Goal: To make some of the children's favorite books available for them to listen and respond to.

Materials:

blank cassette tape
tape recorder and mike
favorite books

Preparations: Make a recording of a favorite book while reading it to the children in a whole group story time. Once the tape is completed, place the book and tape in the Listening Center and encourage the children to listen to the story again on tape while following along with the book.

Notes: Choose a predictable book to read and encourage the children to say the lines they know along with you. They will look forward to hearing themselves on tape in the Listening Center.

Recordings

Goal:

To make a tape recording of each child in the classroom over the course of the entire school year to assess literacy development and for children to enjoy listening to themselves and classmates reading favorite books.

Materials:

blank cassette tape
peel-off file folder label
marker
mailbox (commercially produced or box covered with Con-Tact™ paper)
tape recorder with mike

Preparations:

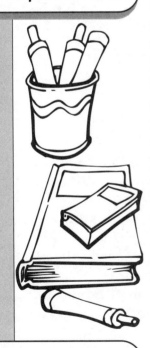

At the beginning of the year, ask each family to send a blank cassette tape to school or add blank cassettes to your classroom supply list. Place a file label on the end of the tape with the child's name printed on it. Once a month, have the children choose a favorite book to read while recording with the tape recorder. At the end of the taping announce the day, month and year. Place the tapes in the mailbox with the labels of names clearly displayed. Children will enjoy listening to themselves and their classmates on tape. Parents may listen to the tapes during a parent/teacher conference. The tape will provide the teacher with an excellent opportunity to discuss the child's literacy development as they hear the child's interpretation of his favorite book. At the end of the school year, the tapes will make an impressive memory of the child's development in language.

Notes:

Ask an older child to assist your children in making their recordings. Schedule a time for the older student to work with the children in the Listening Center during work time.

The Sound Tape

Goal:

To develop a child's ability to listen and identify sounds from a poster of pictures.

Materials:

blank cassette tape
tape recorder and mike
headphones
poster board
various pictures cut from
  magazines
glue
markers
laminating film or clear
  adhesive paper

Preparations:

Record a tape of commonly heard sounds, identifiable by your children. For example: a doorbell, a car horn, a sneeze and a dog barking. Cut pictures from magazines that will correspond to the sounds on the tape in a random sequence from the order on the tape. Glue the pictures on the poster board and print the name under each. Laminate for durability. Place the poster, tape player, cassette and headphones in the Listening Center. Children may listen to the tape and use the poster to identify the sounds they heard.

Notes:

Children may wish to make their own sound tape at home and bring it to the Listening Center to challenge classmates to identify the sounds. Make a label for the cassette tape with the child's name for identification. Encourage the child to find pictures in a magazine to correspond to the recorded sound.

Sounds of Nature

Goal: An opportunity for children to identify sounds in nature after the experience of a walk outside.

Materials:

tape recorder and mike
blank cassette tape
headphones

Preparations: Take the children on a nature walk with a tape recorder and blank cassette tape. Tape the sounds that you hear along the way and discuss the various sounds. For example: birds, leaves rustling in the wind or the sounds your feet make walking along a rocky path. Place the tape in the Listening Center for children to listen to and recall various points of interest and sites from the walk.

Notes: Encourage each child to make a picture of the walk outside while listening to the tape.

Listening and Art

Goal:

To develop music appreciation in children by playing music to listen to as they create a piece of artwork in interpretation.

Materials:

a tape of music (commercially produced or recorded from another source)
tape recorder
headphones
poster board
markers
art materials: paper, crayons, watercolors, etc.

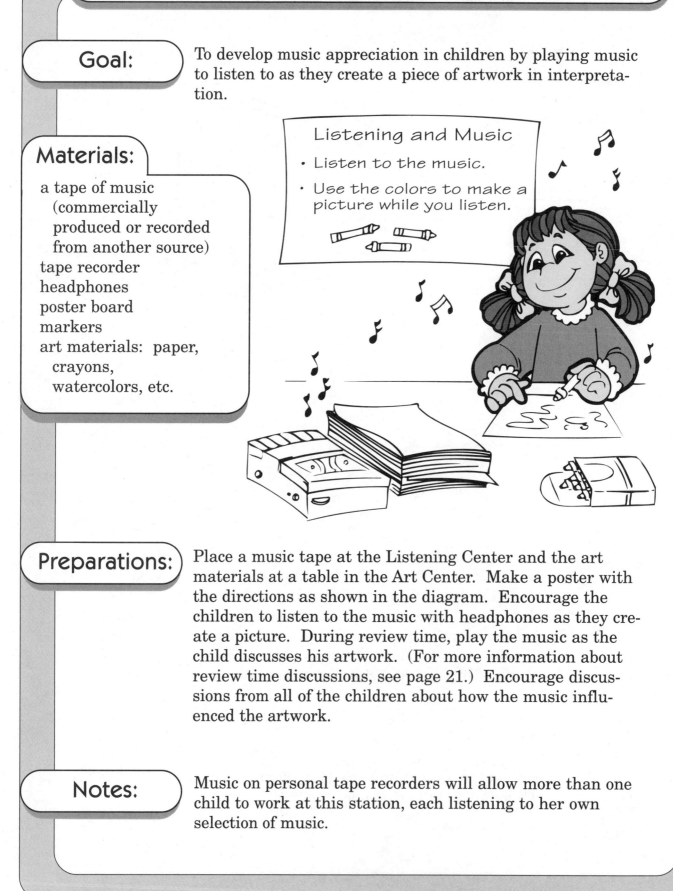

Listening and Music
- Listen to the music.
- Use the colors to make a picture while you listen.

Preparations:

Place a music tape at the Listening Center and the art materials at a table in the Art Center. Make a poster with the directions as shown in the diagram. Encourage the children to listen to the music with headphones as they create a picture. During review time, play the music as the child discusses his artwork. (For more information about review time discussions, see page 21.) Encourage discussions from all of the children about how the music influenced the artwork.

Notes:

Music on personal tape recorders will allow more than one child to work at this station, each listening to her own selection of music.

Listening Graph

Goal: Children will respond verbally to a question and compare their answers to those of classmates.

Materials:
blank cassette tape
tape recorder and mike
poster board
markers

Listening Graph
Tell us about your birthday plans.
Miguel
Justin
Kiya
Deb
Mari

Preparations: Record an open-ended question that encourages children to discuss their ideas on a blank cassette tape. For example: "Tell us about your plans for your birthday" or "What do you do to get ready to come to school each day?" Print the question on a piece of poster board and mount it above the tape recorder. Place the tape with the question in the tape recorder. If necessary, demonstrate how to listen to the question and record an answer, or ask an older child or parent volunteer to assist the children in the Listening Center. Encourage children to record their name and response to the question. Children may then listen to the tape to hear how their classmates responded. Use a poster board chart to graph the responses. The Listening Graph may be used for subsequent discussions about the results and to reinforce graphing concepts.

Notes: Allow the children to pose questions for the Listening Graph. Begin the recording by saying; "This is Matthew's question." Then allow the child to record his question.

Group Story

Goal:

To provide a cooperative project for children to develop the concept of a story and record the results.

Materials:

poster
blank cassette tape
tape recorder and mike

Preparations:

Choose a poster that is interesting to the children and that stimulates possibilities for stories. Educational or children's magazines often provide interesting posters that will be suitable for this task. To help give the children the idea of developing a story in a group, you may wish to use the poster to explore creating a story with the entire class. Allow the children to add their ideas to the story. Place the poster in the Listening Center with a tape recorder and blank tape. Encourage the children, working in small groups, to use the picture to create an oral story. When they feel they are ready, tape the story as the children retell it. Let the children name their story and put a label on the tape with their story title. Other children may be encouraged to listen to the story on tape.

Notes:

Older children may first write and illustrate their story before recording it on tape. Once it is recorded, the written version, illustrations and tape may be stored in the Listening Center in a Ziploc™ bag. Copies of the story and tape may be sent home for parents to enjoy, or offer to exchange taped stories with another classroom.

Music Performance Tape

Goal:
To provide the children with the music they are preparing for a muscial performance for listening, enjoying and practice if necessary.

Materials:
blank tape cassette
tape recorder and mike

Preparations:
Make a tape of the songs to be performed for an upcoming musical performance for parents. Make a tape of the children singing during a practice session. Place the tape in the tape recorder located in the Listening Center. The children will enjoy listening to themselves singing on the tape and may wish to sing along to reinforce the music and words.

Notes:
After the performance, allow the children to check out the tape with a library card to take home. Their families will enjoy listening to the music again and they may also wish to make their own duplicate copy for family members who were unable to attend the performance. Additionally, families could take their copy of the tape on a car trip for singing in the car. If possible, provide the families with a written copy of the words to each song on the tape.

The Woodworking Center

The Woodworking Center is a busy construction area where children explore tools and materials. This center may be the first opportunity for many young children to build with real tools and wood. The placement of this center should be where the noise will not distract the other centers. You could consider placing it near the Art Center or, for climates that will accommodate, just outside the classroom on a covered patio-type area. For safety and working conditions, two or three children working in this center is the most you will want to allow at one time.

The key piece of furniture for the Woodworking Center is the work table. The commercially produced work tables are expensive but safe and durable. Any attempt to make your own version should consider duplicating these features.

The Woodworking Center

Justification for the Woodworking Center

Mount a sign in the Woodworking Center at an adult's eye level that states why you have made the educational decision to have a Woodworking Center in your classroom.

The purpose of the Woodworking Center is to give children an opportunity to work with tools and materials to create their own designs. We will observe children using coordination as they hammer, saw and nail. Safety is a primary concern. Learning to use tools safely is an important concept that is developed in the Woodworking Center and one that children will use for the rest of their lives. Children take great pride in making even the simplest creation and that feeling serves to increase their self-esteem.

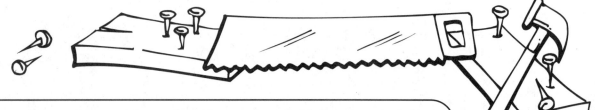

Objectives That May Be Developed in Activities

- Coordination skills, such as eye-hand and small motor, will be developed as children explore the use of the tools.

- Seeing a project develop from a plan or idea to completion is a rewarding and important problem-solving skill.

- Tools and materials are arranged in a way that helps children develop visual matching skills as they go through the process of using and returning materials to their storage place.

- Measuring and making calculations are involved with woodworking projects and develop important mathematical skills in a very practical way.

- Some woodworking projects cause children to encounter unforeseen problems and frustrations. These types of experiences will help young children develop the disposition to persist with a project and the reward of seeing it through to completion.

- Working safely with tools and materials is an important lifetime skill.

The Woodworking Center

The Woodworking Center Materials

The organization of the tools in the Woodworking Center is critical to its success. Mount pegboard at a level that is appropriate for your children. Place the tools on pegboard hooks. To help the children return the tools to their positions, draw an outline of each tool on plain-colored adhesive paper. Adhere the paper to the pegboard.

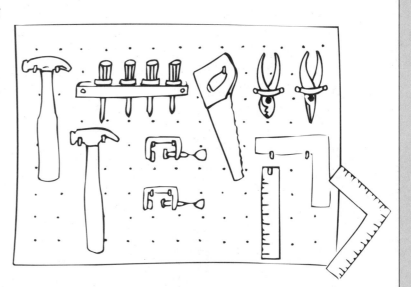

Wood Pieces

A sturdy box or tub should be readily available with wood scraps and pieces. Check with your local lumberyard to see if they might supply the classroom with wood scraps.

The Woodworking Center

The Woodworking Center Materials

Add a shelf with other materials useful to the Woodworking Center, such as sandpaper, various types of glue and a divided container with nuts and bolts.

Add paints and paintbrushes to the materials stored in the Woodworking Center for children to use for painting their projects.

Child-size safety goggles will help reinforce the safety concerns that you will be demonstrating for young children in the Woodworking Center. They should be available in your local school supply catalog.

The Woodworking Center

The Woodworking Center Materials

Place graph paper and colored pencils in the Woodworking Center for drawing designs for projects.

Tasks in the Woodworking Center

Tasks are added to the basic materials in a learning center to enhance the experience for the children. Begin the Woodworking Center with the basic materials and then add new tasks, one at a time. These tasks are designed to be child-directed. The titles tell you the following:

Task: The name of the new collection of materials to be added to the center.

Goal: One possible skill, knowledge or disposition children may develop as a result of this experience.

Materials: Materials you will need to collect for this task.

Preparations: A description of the preparations you will need to make before you present the task into the learning center.

Notes: Follow-up or additional ideas of things children may do as a result of this experience. For example:

Hammer Time

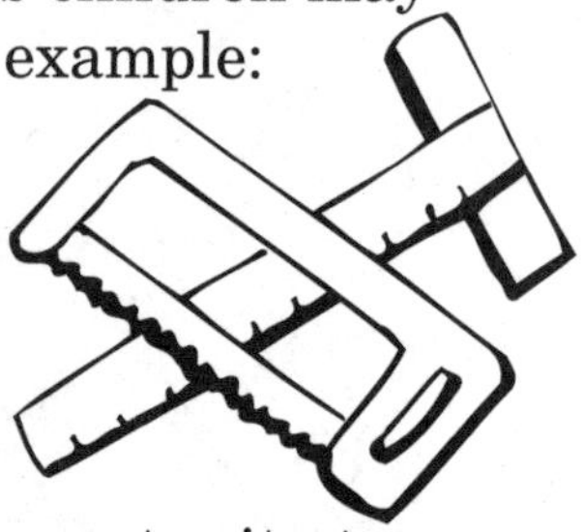

Goal: Work with a hammer and nail provides an opportunity to develop eye-hand coordination.

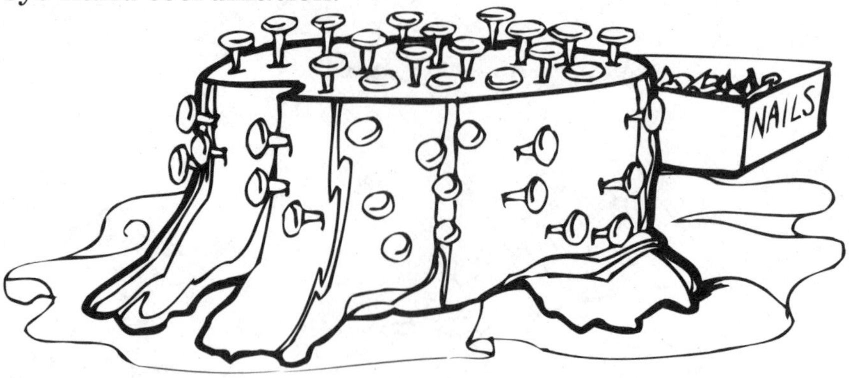

Materials:

large stump
plastic drop cloth
box of nails with label
hammer

Preparations: A parent or school volunteer may be able to assist you in locating and delivering a stump to the classroom. Be sure to clean it as much as possible, and place the stump on the plastic drop cloth. Add a box of nails and several small hammers. With adult supervision, allow the children to hammer nails into the stump.

Notes: It is a great eye-hand coordination exercise to use the claw on the hammer to remove the nails at the end of work time.

Styrofoam™ Working

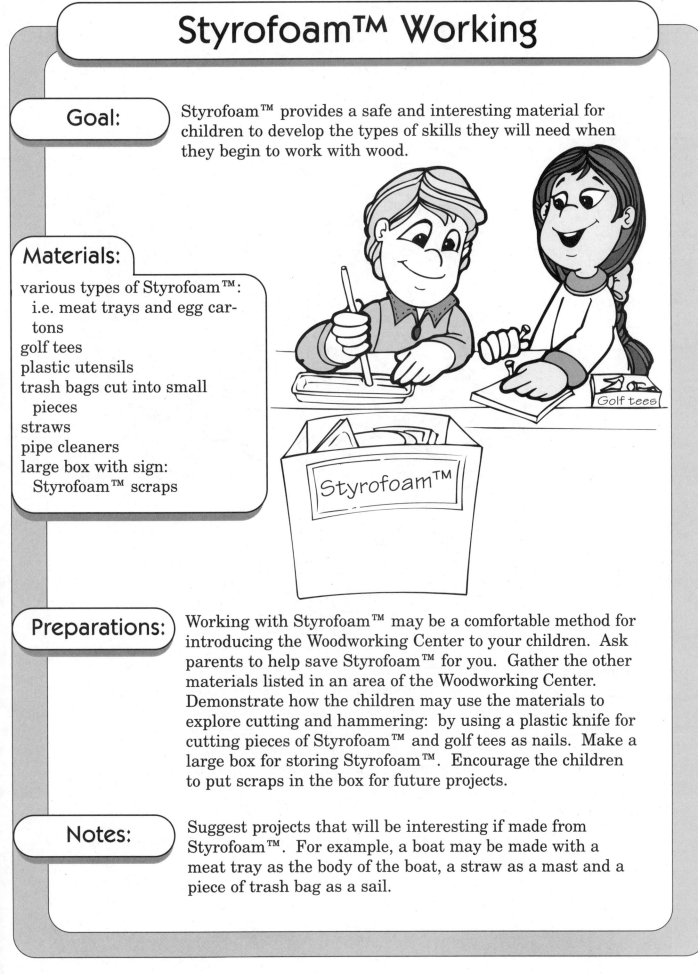

Goal: Styrofoam™ provides a safe and interesting material for children to develop the types of skills they will need when they begin to work with wood.

Materials:

various types of Styrofoam™:
  i.e. meat trays and egg cartons
golf tees
plastic utensils
trash bags cut into small
  pieces
straws
pipe cleaners
large box with sign:
  Styrofoam™ scraps

Golf tees

Styrofoam™

Preparations: Working with Styrofoam™ may be a comfortable method for introducing the Woodworking Center to your children. Ask parents to help save Styrofoam™ for you. Gather the other materials listed in an area of the Woodworking Center. Demonstrate how the children may use the materials to explore cutting and hammering: by using a plastic knife for cutting pieces of Styrofoam™ and golf tees as nails. Make a large box for storing Styrofoam™. Encourage the children to put scraps in the box for future projects.

Notes: Suggest projects that will be interesting if made from Styrofoam™. For example, a boat may be made with a meat tray as the body of the boat, a straw as a mast and a piece of trash bag as a sail.

Using a Screwdriver

Goal:
To give children practice in using a screwdiver for developing eye-hand coordination and help children think about projects where they may use similar materials.

Materials:
pieces of wood
sandpaper
medium-sized screws
several screwdrivers

Preparations:

Create a practice board for using a screwdriver by drilling holes in a well-sanded piece of soft wood. Use an electric drill to get the hole started for a screw. Then place medium-sized screws and several sizes of screwdrivers with the practice board. Children may find that they need to work with a friend to help hold the board as they place the screws in the board.

Notes:
Add screws to the materials in the Woodworking Center for future projects.

Mitre Box

Goal: A mitre box is an ideal method for assisting children who wish to experiment with cutting wood with a saw.

Materials:

three pieces of wood
nails
hammer
saw
pieces of wood or
   branches to be cut

Preparations: Prepare a mitre box by using three pieces of wood, cut the same size to form a box as shown in the diagram. Cut identical slits in the two sides for holding the material to be cut. Gather various types of wood that will allow children to practice cutting. Branches from tree limbs make a good practice material. Demonstrate safety rules in regard to using the saw. Encourage the children to work carefully cutting wood. Leave the mitre box in the center for projects they are making that require cutting.

Notes: After the children have practiced cutting with the mitre box, introduce the project of the Bird Feeder on page 99 which requires cutting a branch.

Frame It

Goal: A project for children to show pride in their artwork by making their own frame and also to provide them with a project that requires the development of sanding skills.

Materials:

pieces of wood
sandpaper
child's artwork (paint-
  ings or collage projects)
wood glue
paper clip

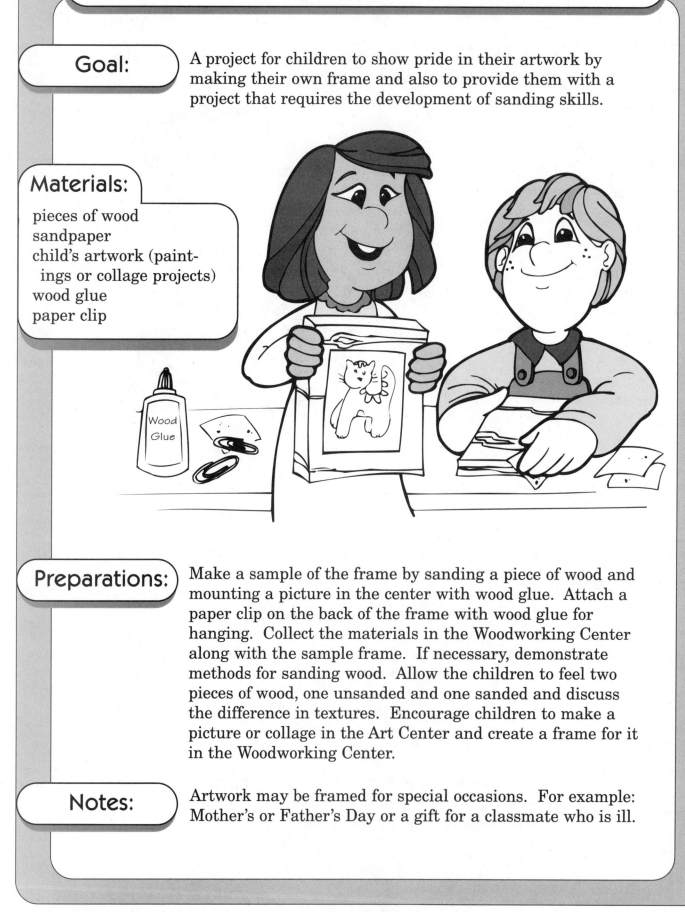

Preparations: Make a sample of the frame by sanding a piece of wood and mounting a picture in the center with wood glue. Attach a paper clip on the back of the frame with wood glue for hanging. Collect the materials in the Woodworking Center along with the sample frame. If necessary, demonstrate methods for sanding wood. Allow the children to feel two pieces of wood, one unsanded and one sanded and discuss the difference in textures. Encourage children to make a picture or collage in the Art Center and create a frame for it in the Woodworking Center.

Notes: Artwork may be framed for special occasions. For example: Mother's or Father's Day or a gift for a classmate who is ill.

Woodworking Recipe

Goal: Children will follow a step-by-step procedure for completing a project to develop concepts about sequencing.

Materials:

oaktag
markers
copies of the patterns
pieces of wood
sandpaper

hammer
hook
yarn
outdoor materials
glue

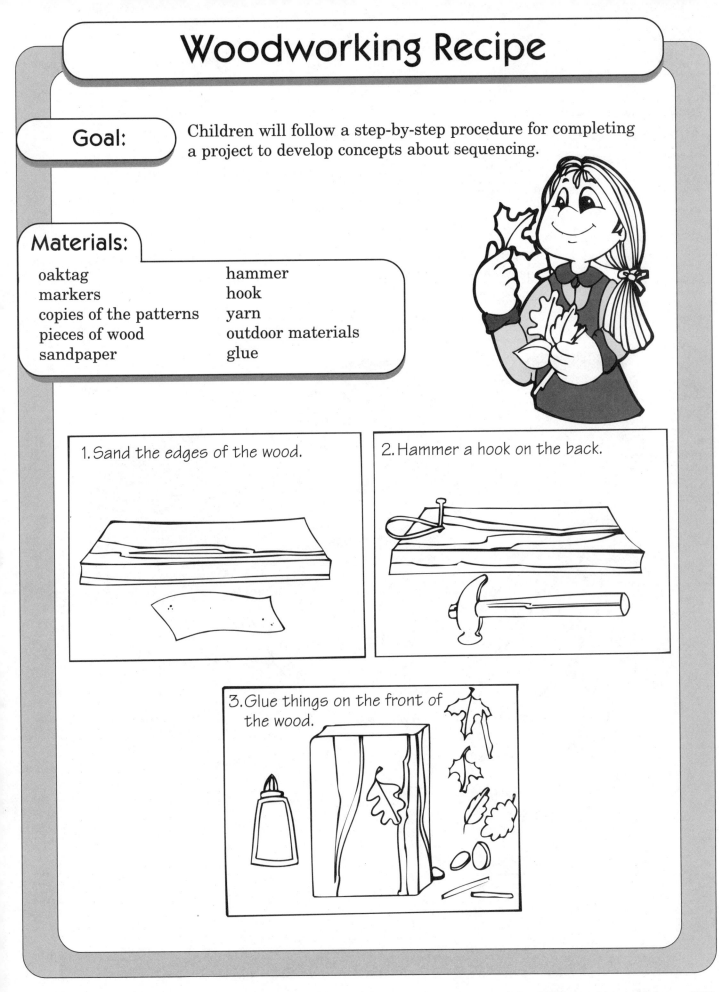

1. Sand the edges of the wood.

2. Hammer a hook on the back.

3. Glue things on the front of the wood.

Woodworking Recipe

Enlarge the following directions onto sheets of oaktag folded so that each can stand alone. Place the cards in order and collect the necessary materials to produce the project of a collage of natural materials.

Notes: Develop other step-by-step projects with directions to add to the Woodworking Center.

Bird Feeder

Goal: Children can make a project that will have a useful function.

Materials:

pieces of wood
various sizes of tree
 branches
twine
saw
glue
hammer
nails

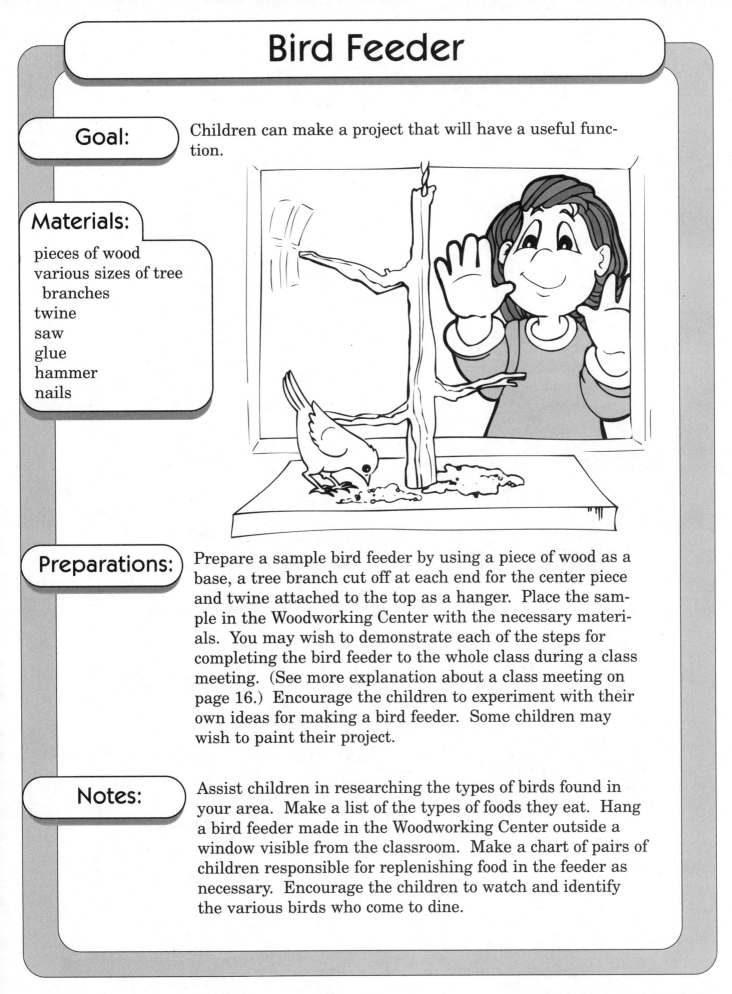

Preparations: Prepare a sample bird feeder by using a piece of wood as a base, a tree branch cut off at each end for the center piece and twine attached to the top as a hanger. Place the sample in the Woodworking Center with the necessary materials. You may wish to demonstrate each of the steps for completing the bird feeder to the whole class during a class meeting. (See more explanation about a class meeting on page 16.) Encourage the children to experiment with their own ideas for making a bird feeder. Some children may wish to paint their project.

Notes: Assist children in researching the types of birds found in your area. Make a list of the types of foods they eat. Hang a bird feeder made in the Woodworking Center outside a window visible from the classroom. Make a chart of pairs of children responsible for replenishing food in the feeder as necessary. Encourage the children to watch and identify the various birds who come to dine.

The Manipulative Center

The Manipulative Center provides children with interesting materials to use for exploration. It is this exploration time that research has found to be beneficial in supporting children's understanding in mathematical and logical thinking. This center creates a cozy corner for housing a variety of manipulative materials by placing a hinged shelf in the middle of the floor and defining the space with a bright rug. This center will accommodate two to four children comfortably.

An ideal piece of furniture to set the stage for the Manipulative Center is a hinged shelf.

The Manipulative Center

Justification for the Manipulative Center

Mount a sign in the Manipulative Center at an adult's eye level that states why you have made the educational decision to have a Manipulative Center in your classroom.

The Manipulative Center is a special place where the children can work with interesting materials. Some materials are introduced to the children in a lesson where they are given ideas of ways to use them. Other materials are placed at the center for children to explore on their own. In both ways, teachers gain insight into how children figure out a variety of math and problem-solving strategies using these materials. We know that young children need to begin math understanding with real materials before they attempt to do the same type of work with numerals on paper. This center makes a variety of math concepts "real" to the children and will help them with any math thinking they will encounter in future work.

Objectives That May Be Developed in Activities

- Math computation skills are reinforced when working with manipulatives, as well as patterning, sequencing, size and measurement.
- Problem-solving skills are enhanced with many of the materials in the Manipulative Center.
- When several children work together in the center, they will often be observed using negotiation skills.
- The categorizing of materials found in the Manipulative Center enhances many skills in mathematical and logical thinking.

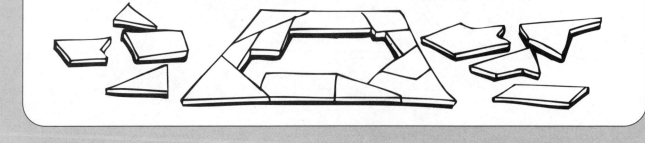

The Manipulative Center

The Manipulative Center Materials

The key to the Manipulative Center is the organization of the materials. See Chapter 3 for more information on the thinking behind this strategy.

A bright colored, low-nap rug offers a sense of boundary to the Manipulative Center. You may purchase them commercially or create your own by asking a local carpet store to supply you with sample pieces. Use heavy electrical tape to attach the pieces together on the back.

The Manipulative Center

The Manipulative Center Materials

A well-stocked supply of commercial manipulatives are important supplies for the Manipulative Center.

Beads

Color Blocks

Tiles

A variety of types and styles of puzzles should be placed in the Manipulative Center.

Floor Puzzle

40 pieces

25 pieces

Tasks in the Manipulative Center

Tasks are added to the basic materials in a learning center to enhance the experience for the children. Begin the Manipulative Center with the basic materials and then add new tasks, one at a time. These tasks are designed to be child-directed. The titles tell you the following:

Task: The name of the new collection of materials to be added to the center.

Goal: One possible skill, knowledge or disposition children may develop as a result of this experience.

Materials: Materials you will need to collect for this task.

Preparations: A description of the preparations you will need to make before you present the task into the learning center.

Notes: Follow-up or additional ideas of things children may do as a result of this experience. For example:

Magnetic Board

Goal: Work with magnetic pieces establishes information for children about magnets, and additionally this task allows children to explore the magnetic pieces creatively.

Materials:

small, white magnetic
   board on an easel
variety of magnetic pieces
small box for storage

Preparations: Collect a variety of magnetic pieces in a box with a label. For example: plain magnets, magnetic strips, plastic shapes and alphabet pieces. Place the magnetic white board on a low table with the box of magnetic pieces and allow ample opportunity for the children to explore.

Notes: Children may work together to create group pictures. After time for exploration, you may wish to provide paper and colored pencils and encourage the children to re-create their designs on paper.

Collection Boxes

Goal:

Collection Boxes are an interesting collection of materials that children help gather. Because of the way they are organized, children find the materials interesting to use on their own to increase their skills in categorization or in conjunction with some other materials in the Manipulative Center.

Materials:

set of small boxes (Children's shoe boxes or check boxes are ideal.)
variety of materials: seashells, rocks, pinecones, old costume jewelry, paper clips, mini cars, etc.
markers

Preparations:

The key to collection boxes is involving the children in gathering the materials. To accomplish this goal, send a letter to parents with a list of materials that they may have at home that they could send to school with their child. Stress to the parents that you would like their child to help in gathering the materials they will be sending. You may also take a nature walk around the school to help find some of the materials. Gather the set of boxes and make a label with the name of the item and a simple picture for each box. Store the boxes on a shelf in the Manipulative Center. When children arrive at school with items for the collection boxes, allow them to work with a friend to sort their things into the boxes by using the name and picture as clues. Use the collection boxes in whole or small group manipulative lessons, and encourage the children to explore the boxes during work time. Include materials from the Collection Boxes with other tasks in the Manipulative Center. For example: Choose several Collection Boxes for use with the Balance Scale (page 109) or the Overhead Projector (page 111).

Shoots and Slides Tub

Goal: Children will explore concepts of motion by experimenting with materials to make a maze for a ball.

Materials:

plastic tub
variety of paper towel tubes
golf or plastic balls
masking tape

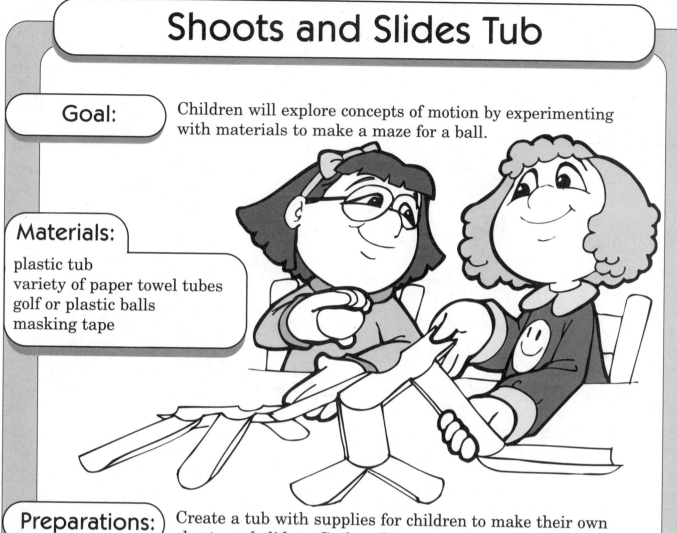

Preparations:

Create a tub with supplies for children to make their own shoots and slides. Gather the materials in a plastic tub. Place a label and picture on the tub that says: "Shoots and Slides." You may wish to ask parents to help collect different types of paper towel tubes. Add several sizes of balls, for example, a golf or plastic ball. Include masking tape in the kit. Encourage the children to tape several tubes together to make a maze for the balls to pass through. Ask a child to bring his completed maze to a review time to share with the other children. Discuss some of the attributes of the maze. For example: How fast did the ball travel? What sections of the maze allowed the ball to go fastest? Can you make a maze that will allow the ball to go up hill? (For additional information about review time discussions, see page 21.)

Notes: Add additional materials to the tub. Some packing pieces that come in boxes, egg cartons and other small boxes will add new interest to the task.

The Pendulum

Goal: Children will explore the concepts of weight and motion by working with a pendulum.

Materials:

dowel rod, approximately 2 feet (.61 cm) long
string
weight (heavy nut or other object that can hang from a string)
variety of empty food boxes

Preparations: Choose an area in the classroom that will allow a clear and safe area for the pendulum to swing. Make the pendulum by hanging a dowel rod from the ceiling with string on each end. Tie a string to the middle of the dowel rod with a weight on the opposite end. The string should hang approximately 1' (.30 m) to 18" (45.72 cm) above the ground. Place some cardboard blocks or empty food boxes next to the pendulum. Children can stack the blocks and experiment with how to swing the pendulum to hit the target. Some challenging questions about their work with the pendulum may show you how their thinking is developing. For example: How high do you need to stack the boxes to knock them down? Can you knock down the boxes on the first swing? What would happen if the weight was higher?

Notes: Add other materials to the pendulum for experimenting and interest. For example: Add empty milk cartons or jugs, plastic or paper cups, or make a target with a large appliance box. Paint or use markers to draw targets on the side for the children to try to hit with the pendulum.

Balance Scale

Goal:
Children will explore concepts of balance when given the opportunity to work with a balance scale.

Materials:

half-gallon milk carton
strip of 3-ply cardboard
longarm paper brad
paper clips
2 Styrofoam™ cups
variety of materials for
    weighing

Preparations:

If you do not have a balance scale to put in your Manipulative Center, you can make an inexpensive one yourself. Use a half-gallon milk carton as the base. Attach a strip of 3-ply cardboard at the center with a sturdy long-arm paper brad. Use paper clips to attach a Styrofoam™ cup to each end of the cardboard strip. Gather a variety of materials for exploration. Children will compare the weights of a variety of items. For weighing, use various dried beans, corn kernels, pennies, paper clips, costume jewelry, small plastic people or Styrofoam™ packing peanuts. Ask the children working with the balance scale questions that will encourage their thinking about weight and balance. For example: Ask the children to make esti-mations. "How many pennies do you think it will take on one side of the scale and lima beans on the other to make the scale even?"

Notes:
Continue to add new materials to the balance scale to increase the knowledge about weights and to continue the interest in working with the scale. For example: Add small plastic block pieces, pinecones, plastic mini cars and seashells. See the Collection Boxes (page 106) for ideas of materials that may be used with the balance scale.

Card Games

Goal:

Children can explore number concepts while playing games with a deck of playing cards. Possible concepts that may be observed in play are combining and subtracting numbers and conventional rules of playing games.

Materials:

an old deck of playing cards

Preparations:

Begin by introducing a deck of cards in the Manipulative Center and watch to see what kinds of games children play and how much they know about playing games with other children. Many card games reinforce math concepts and provide an ideal forum for observing skills. One game that young children enjoy is War. Remove the face cards from several decks of cards. Two children may play at one time. Divide the deck evenly among the children and place the cards facedown. Children turn over their top card simultaneously and compare the two to see who has the higher number. The higher number keeps both cards. The game ends when one child runs out of cards.

Notes:

The teacher may observe the play for assessment in number recognition.

Overhead Projector

Goal: An overhead projector makes a very appealing task for young children to explore the concepts of materials and light.

Materials:

overhead projector
screen
variety of materials that are transparent to light: glass, clear plastic pieces
variety of materials that are not transparent: paper clips, pennies, cardboard shapes
transparency (overhead projector film) pages
overhead projector pens

Preparations: Place the projector on a solid surface with a screen area at the child's eye level. Collect a variety of objects for children to explore. Allow the children to explore the materials on the overhead projector. Add the transparencies and markers to the materials and allow the children to make their own pictures that they can show on the screen to others.

Notes: Add yarn to the materials at the overhead projector, tied in large circles for children to make number groupings on the overhead projector.

Money Box

Goal: The Money Box allows the children an opportunity to explore paper and coins and incorporate them into other center tasks.

Materials:

plastic tub with a
   label and picture
play paper money and
   coins
cents-off coupons
money stamps and
   stamp pad
paper

Preparations: Create the Money Box by placing the materials in a plastic tub. The money stamps and paper will allow the children to make their own money. Allow ample time for the children to explore the Money Box without expectations of types of denominations or values attached. Encourage the children to use the Money Box with other center tasks. For example: If children are interested in setting up a store area in the room, and express and need for money, remind them of the Money Box in the Manipulative Center.

Notes: A toy cash register will add a new level of interest to the Money Box.

The Dramatic Play Center

The Dramatic Play Center is the social area of the classroom. Young children are interested in trying out the roles, often patterned after the adults around them. In the Dramatic Play Center they may begin with the roles they see in their home environments. Begin the set up of the Dramatic Play Center with the home setup as shown in the diagram. The kitchen set, baby bed and mirror are the traditional materials associated with the home setup of the Dramatic Play Center. This is an active, busy center, and the organization of the materials must reflect this goal. Talking and moving are to be expected. Because of this, you may want to place this center in an area that is near other busy centers like the Block Center, where an interchange of similar materials and activity will support each other.

The Dramatic Play Center

Justification for the Dramatic Play Center

Mount a sign in the Dramatic Play Center at an adult's eye level that states why you have made the educational decision to have a Dramatic Play Center in your classroom.

The Dramatic Play Center allows children to re-create the social roles they see in their everyday lives. The setup of the center is designed to encourage children to try out the roles of parents, children and workers. Communicating with other children is a key skill that we will see in the work at the center. As the year progresses, the Dramatic Play Center will change and evolve to reflect the themes and interest of the children. After a field trip to a grocery store, for example, the children may change the Dramatic Play Center into a grocery store of their own that they will run. From this type of activity, we will see what they have discovered about the workers and shoppers in a store.

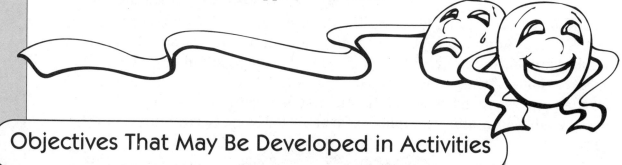

Objectives That May Be Developed in Activities

- Social skills such as communicating, negotiating and problem solving are key skills developed.
- The Dramatic Play Center involves representational skills, ones where children show us what they know about and where their interests lie.
- Depending on the setup of the Dramatic Play Center, children will use counting, sorting and other mathematical skills during their work time.
- A well-designed center allows children to use skills of logic and categorizing while taking care of the materials in the center.

The Dramatic Play Center

The Dramatic Play Center Materials

Dress-up clothes stored in well-labeled drawers or on easily accessible hooks add interest to the Dramatic Play Center.

A child-sized table provides a multitude of possibilities for the Dramatic Play Center. Add plates, cups, utensils, pots and pans for simulating cooking and eating activities. Educational resource suppliers have child-sized versions of these materials, or visit a few garage or yard sales and purchase an inexpensive set of plastic dishes. You may also add place mats, a tablecloth and a simple centerpiece for some extra touches to the center.

The Dramatic Play Center

The Dramatic Play Center Materials

Children are interested in using real materials. Ask parents or school volunteers to save empty food boxes to stock the cupboards of the Dramatic Play Center.

Other basic materials that are important to the setup of the Dramatic Play Center include a telephone, iron, toaster and cash register. Other simple appliances that children would expect to find in a home may be added. Many educational supply companies make toy versions of these materials, but you may choose to add real ones from a garage sale.

Tasks in the Dramatic Play Center

Tasks are added to the basic materials in a learning center to enhance the experience for the children. Begin the Dramatic Play Center with the basic materials and then add new tasks, one at a time. These tasks are designed to be child-directed. The titles tell you the following:

Task: The name of the new collection of materials to be added to the center.

Goal: One possible skill, knowledge or disposition children may develop as a result of this experience.

Materials: Materials you will need to collect for this task.

Preparations: A description of the preparations you will need to make before you present the task into the learning center.

Notes: Follow-up or additional ideas of things children may do as a result of this experience. For example:

Puppet Theater

Goal: To allow children to explore creating their own ideas about stories and characters with puppets.

Materials:

appliance box
tempera paint
brushes
X-acto knife

Preparations: Cut the flaps off of the appliance box and cut a door in the back and a window in front. Allow the children to paint and decorate the box as they would like. Place commercial or child-created puppets in the theater, and encourage the children to make their own plays.

Notes: Children may add props with materials at the Art Center.

Prop Boxes

Goal: Prop boxes incorporate classroom themes or interests of children as they learn more about the area of study.

Materials:

large plastic storage
  tubs with lids
oaktag
markers
theme-related materials

Preparations: Prepare the prop box with a label cut from oaktag that names the theme materials that will be stored in the tub. Collect materials for an upcoming theme in the tub. For example: In a tub for a farm theme, you might gather several books about the farm; a work hat, vest or other related clothing; miniature farm equipment, animals, barn, fence, etc. Introduce the theme with the prop box. At a class meeting or other whole group time, the children can explore the tub and identify the materials you have gathered. Read one of the books on the theme. Place the tub in the Dramatic Play Center so that the children may incorporate the materials into the play at the center.

Notes: Add to the prop box as the theme progresses. Children may find related materials at home that they wish to contribute. Take a trip to the library or a local museum for materials that fit with the theme. Write a class book about the theme and add it to the prop box.

Writing in the Dramatic Play Center

Goal: By adding a variety of authentic writing materials to the Dramatic Play Center, the children's play will become more realistic.

Materials:

variety of writing supplies: food order pads, telephone message pads, lined paper, bookkeepers notebook, etc.
pencils, pens and markers
variety of other papers: oaktag, poster board, gift wrap and construction paper

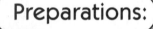
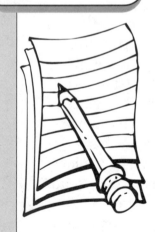

Preparations: Writing materials may be added to the Dramatic Play Center as the activity of the children dictates. For example: If you observe a child talking on the telephone, bring a telephone message pad to her and suggest she may wish to "take a message." Alternately, you may also add a set of writing materials to the center materials and suggest their use when it seems appropriate. The other types of paper suggested in the materials list will be interesting to keep at the center for a variety of uses. Children may wish to make a sign for a special area, write a note or grocery list, or wrap a gift for a special occasion they are pretending to celebrate in the Dramatic Play Center.

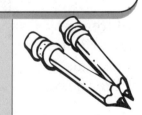

Notes: As the Dramatic Play Center evolves during the year and becomes different settings, the types of writing materials may change as well. For example: If children set up the center to become a fast food restaurant, children may need signs for the customers, order pads and labels for food shelves. Encourage the children to discuss the signs they need and assist each other in making them.

Face Painting

Goal: Children will explore their own creativity and make discoveries about the ways they are alike and different from other children.

Materials:

floor-length mirror
muffin tin
cotton swabs
face paint
facial cream
tissues
place mats

Preparations: Prepare a face painting area in the Dramatic Play Center by placing a floor-length mirror horizontally across a wall with a table in front of it. Gather the materials listed. Place a small amount of various colors of face paint in muffin tins. (Face paint may be purchased in costume or craft stores.) Make two or three stations at the table for children to work, depending on the size of the table. Designate the stations with a place mat for each. Demonstrate some procedures for using the materials. For example: Using the cotton swab for applying a small amount of paint to the face and removing the paint with the facial cream and a tissue. Encourage children to explore various techniques and characters with the paint. Pictures of clown faces posted on the mirror may encourage exploration.

Notes: Challenge two children to make matching faces to encourage them to work together and to study each other as they work.

The Hospital

Goal:

Children will explore the various roles they know about in a hospital setting and work with relevant materials.

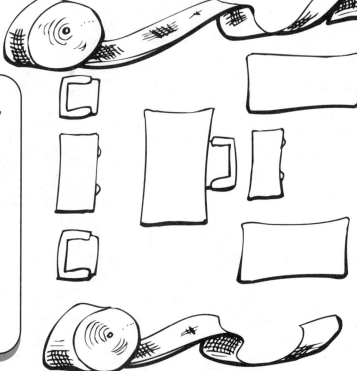

Materials:

2 child-sized cots
various medical supplies: bandages,
  empty medicine bottles, white lab
  coats or men's shirts
magazines
scale
height chart
clipboard
poster board
markers
large sheet
telephone
paper and pencils

Preparations:

Prepare the hospital using the diagram above as a guide. Designate two areas with a sheet hung between the reception and patient areas. Set up the reception area with a small desk for the receptionist and materials such as a telephone, clipboard, paper and pencils. Use a small chest (or substitute the Dramatic Play area furniture, such as the stove) for magazines. In the patient area, set up two cots with a chest between them to hold medical supplies. Check with a local doctor, pharmacy or a parent who works in the health care profession for a donation of additional materials that would be safe and interesting for children to explore. Add the white lab jackets or men's shirts to allow the children to complete the scene with their dress. Encourage the children to make any signs they feel necessary for the hospital, using the poster board and markers.

Notes:

To encourage opportunities for writing and gathering information, add a simple form for the receptionist to use as patients check into the hospital.

Play Dough Station

Goal: Opportunities for children to make a variety of props for the Dramatic Play Center.

Materials:

large plastic tub
container of play dough, either commercial or teacher-made
cookie cutters
rolling pins
plastic utensils
small plastic containers with lids
plastic place mats

Preparations: Gather the materials described above into a large plastic tub with a label on the front. Introduce the tub to the children in a class meeting or to a small group of children who are working in the Dramatic Play Center. Encourage the children to work with the materials at a table on the place mats. Children may find it interesting to make food for their kitchen work, use lumps of play dough for holding signs in a store or pretend to work in a bakery.

Notes: Add additional materials to the tub as the work of the children dictates or that you feel they will find interesting. Various odds and ends for making imprints will add new interest to the tub. For example: a potato masher, plastic drinking cups in a variety of sizes and plastic gears.

The Office

Goal:

To create an area for children to explore the roles they associate with workers in offices and to develop written and communication skills.

Materials:

- small desk and chair
- typewriter or computer
- telephone
- cardboard mailboxes
- "junk mail"
- paper and pencils
- pencil holder
- clipboard
- typing paper
- desk blotter
- in/out box
- suit jacket

Preparations:

Prepare the office in the Dramatic Play Center using the picture above as a guide and adding as many of your own realistic touches as possible. If an old or used adult desk is available, ask a maintenance worker to remove the legs. Seated flat on the floor, the desk will feel "real" to the children but be at a more convenient level for them. Add a typewriter or computer on a small desk or typing table. Other writing materials will provide the work for the office and a few dress-up clothes will add to the realism.

Notes:

Take the children on a visit to some of the offices located throughout the school. Suggest they take notes about the kinds of materials they find in each of the offices and discuss the possibility of gaining similar materials for their office. Make a list of the suggestions and check them off as the children feel they have found something that will work.

Chapter 11
Assessment, Record Keeping and Parent Conferences

This chapter is designed to provide information in assessing the work that children do during their work time in learning centers, how to keep track of all of the information you learn while they are working and the important communication that you have with the parents. In other words, this chapter will answer three key questions:

What do children know, need to know or what knowledge are they still developing?

How do you document what you find out?

What do you know about the children that you can share with parents?

Formal assessments (for example, standardize tests) are designed by someone other than yourself and often tell you only a limited part of what you want to know about children's knowledge. With learning centers, you have the opportunity to design your own assessment program that will prove more meaningful for you and the families of the children.

The assessment program that you design should match the philosophy that is in place in your classroom. In Chapter 1 of this book, the philosophy that is offered for using learning centers is one of development. A developmental assessment program requires you to look at the following:

What do children know?
What have they figured out?
How did they figure out what they know?

Each of those questions should be answered for all four areas of the child's development:
Cognitive
Language
Physical
Social/Emotional

An Assessment Program for Learning Centers

You have a dual role as the teacher during the work time:

Observing the children in their centers. While the children work with the various materials in the centers their work and the processes they go through while they work, provide you with information in each of the four areas of development.

An example:

You observe a child who is attempting to build a tower with blocks. He places several larger blocks on the top of the tower and the entire structure falls down. As you continue to observe his work, you will learn whether or not the child will persist with his goal of building the high tower. Will he make the same mistake again, or will he figure out that the structure will be more secure if he starts with larger blocks on the bottom?

An Assessment Program for Learning Centers

Questioning children during their work in centers is the second part of your assessment program. Informal questions asked of children while they work with another child or with some materials in the learning center will give you ideas about how children think and work out the problems they encounter.

An example:

While watching a child who is working a puzzle, you observe that she is very randomly picking up two pieces to see if they fit together. If they do not, she drops them and chooses another two. You ask her: "Would there be another way to find which pieces fit together?" The question may begin a conversation about strategies for working puzzles, or you may return to observing the child to see if your question promoted some new thinking for her that will result in a new strategy for working a puzzle.

Observation Records

The following are ideas for recording your observations of children in learning centers. Choose one of these or design one that you feel comfortable implementing in your classroom.

Keep a spiral notebook with each child's name on a page. Place several sheets of peel-off labels in each center. As you observe a child, make a note on one of the labels. At the end of the day, collect the labels and stick notes about each child on his page in the spiral notebook. Print the date beside the label.

Use an index card for writing observations about each child. Place the date at the top of the card. At the end of the day, file the cards in a card file or in the child's portfolio file.

Observation Records

Duplicate a list of the names of the children in the classroom on one sheet of paper. Leave space between each name. Place several copies of the list on clipboards and hang the clipboards at the adult's eye level in each learning center. Use the list to make quick reminder notes as you make observations in each center. At the end of the day collect the notes and transcribe them to a notebook or index cards to be placed in the child's portfolio.

Questioning Records

These ideas are designed to help you in recording conversations you have as you question children during their work in learning centers or discussions that result during your questions to the children at the review time. (For more information about review time, see page 21.)

Keep a clipboard and paper with you during the review time. You may make a form with a list of the children's names and space for recording quick notes about some of the information gained from your questions about their work at centers.

When you add a new task to a learning center, take a few minutes to write a few questions that you might ask about the materials. For example: Some questions about the Balance Scale (page 109). How will you know if the scale is balanced? Are pennies heavier than the beans? How many corn kernels do you think it would take to balance the scale if you put two paper clips in the cup?

Make tape recordings of conversations you have with a child in a learning center as he describes an art project, a book he has made or while he is reading a favorite story. (See the task in the Listening Center, Recordings page 79.)

Collecting Information About Children

The following are methods for collecting information about individual children.

Literacy Folders: Dated samples of drawings, other types of artwork and writing, collected regularly.

Reading Tapes: Begin with emergent readers. Once a month, the child chooses a favorite book to read on his own blank tape.

Teacher Observations: Focus on one child as often as possible during one day, and make notes on both language and content. Use as much descriptive language in your notes as possible.

Observation in Daily Living Situations: Focus on one activity and make notes on how various children approach the task. For example: setting the table for snack time.

Observation in Group Games: Choose a specific game to play with every child in the class, one or two at a time. Record the information systematically on a form made for this purpose.

Individual Interviews: Use quiet areas of the room to talk privately with one child. Assess her ability to problem solve and use logic.

Journals and Notebooks: Encourage the children to write their own ideas, scores from games, observations from science experiments or list of favorite books.

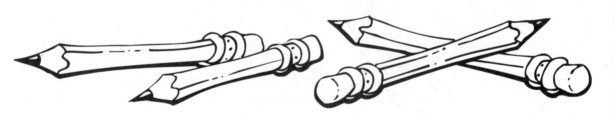

Adapted from "Achievement Testing in the Early Grades: The Games Grown-Ups Play," Constance Kamii, Ed., NAEYC; Washington, DC, 1990.

Observing Social Situations in Learning Centers

You can learn a great deal about a child's social development in a learning center.

For example:

While children play games, you may observe:

How do the players decide who will go first?
Do the children take turns, and what happens when someone goes out of turn?
Do the children change the rules of the game?
How do the children declare a winner, and do the players accept the winner?

Observing Social Situations in Learning Centers

When children are working together on a project, you may observe:

How do they decide who will work together?
What roles do the children take in the project?
How do they resolve any conflicts?
Can they reach a common goal?

Portfolio Assessment

A portfolio assessment program is a collection of children's work. The teacher's role is to compare the work of the child over a period of time to see how the child's skills are developing. For example, if you collect a sample of a child's writing once a month, when you compare several months you will find out how the writing process is developing for that child. This assessment is easy to explain to parents. With samples of their child's work, they can see the development.

Early in the school year, discuss with the children the idea of a special file where they will keep some of their best work. The more the children understand that a file of their work is a way of showing their parents what they are learning, the more they will become interested in adding to their collection. Collecting samples of all types of work should be a daily part of your program.

Set up a place for collecting a variety of work from children. A hanging file system is an ideal way to have easy access for you and the children.

Portfolio Assessment

Purchase a date stamp and ink pad. Keep them close to the files and demonstrate to the children how to stamp the date on any work that you agree should go into the file.

Toward the end of the school year ask each child to help you sort through his file. Make three piles of the work collected. One pile of work that you and the child think should be sent on to the next teacher he will have, one of the work to send home to show his parents and the third for a few special things that you will keep.

Communicating with Parents

Regularly scheduled meetings with parents to share your observations are critical to the parents' understanding of their child's development and of your program. During a meeting with parents, your discussions about learning centers should include:

- The child's portfolio of work from learning centers and your evaluation of the child's development.

- Your observations of the child in the learning centers work and what those observations tell you about what the child knows, how he figures things out, where he has developed interest and how he interacts with other children.

- Questions to the parents about their impressions of their child's feelings about school, her self-esteem and interests at home.

Communicating with Parents

The following are other key ways to communicate with parents:

- Send a letter to parents before the school year begins to explain how you use learning centers. Include a list of the centers and the justification for why you have each area in your room. (A justification for each learning center is located at the beginning of each learning center chapter in this book.)

- Offer a time for children to visit school with their parents before the opening day. Set up some special activities for the children in several of the learning centers and while the children work, discuss with the parents the types of things you will be able to observe.

- Hold an open house for parents on an evening shortly after the beginning of the school year. Introduce the learning centers. Demonstrate some of the tasks that their children are doing or, better yet, allow the parents to actually work in the centers. Afterwards, conduct a review time with the parents.

- Send home a montly newsletter with information about new tasks you have added to the learning centers. You may use this opportunity to suggest some materials that parents can save at home for various center work.

- Invite parents to drop by to observe their child working in learning centers or to volunteer to work in the room.